Salient Points
Cameos of the Western Front
Ypres Sector 1914 -1918

To George.

All the best for your
birthday!

Best wishes.

Tony Stagnal.

July 2000.

Tower of Ypres, a little slept your glory
Lips again are busy with your name
Ypres again is famous in our story
Ypres of Flanders, wrapt in blood and flame.

-Everard Owen.

Salient Points
Cameos of the Western Front
Ypres Sector 1914-1918

by
Tony Spagnoly

Edited by
Ted Smith
with an introduction by
Jonathan Nicholls

LEO COOPER

By the same authors:
The Anatomy of a Raid
Australians at Celtic Wood, October 9th 1917

First Published in 1995
Reprinted 1998 by
LEO COOPER
an imprint of
Pen & Sword Books Ltd
47 Church Street, Barnsley, South Yorkshire S70 2AS

Front Cover design by Jim Ludden.

A CIP catalogue record for this book is available
from the British Library.

ISBN 0–85052–319–2

Typeset by IMCC Ltd. in 11/12 point Garamond Light.

Printed in Great Britain by
Redwood Books, Trowbridge, Wiltshire

CONTENTS

LIST OF PLATES

LIST OF MAPS/ILLUSTRATIONS

The last page of each Cameo features a map which is a faithful rendering of the area refered to in the story as it is today. Farms, woodland and areas that exist today are identified by the military names given to them by cartographers of the time. Those farms, woodlands and areas that no longer exist are identified as "Site of.... ". Other maps and sketches appearing within the Cameo texts are shown below.

To my friend Lyn Macdonald who suggested
Salient Points in the first place.

This book is a tribute to all those who lie at Ypres.

He rests in the sunshine
of perpetual peace

Inscription on a Canadian grave at Ypres

ACKNOWLEDGEMENTS

The basic premise of this book is to keep alive the spirit of remembrance. This is the motive which underlies our visits to the general area we emotively know as the Ypres Salient ...the Immortal Salient. Remembrance may not be a top priority concept among our compatriots today, but those who visit Ypres in ever increasing-numbers are more than aware that here is where "the ghosts of great armies dwell" as Jonathan Nicholls penned so superbly in his introduction to this book.

Ypres has a special magic of its own which we are not always able to handle. No matter how many times we stand at the Menin Gate and let the poignant notes of the Last Post drift over us, our worldly problems become insignificant for a moment in time, and we almost become a part of another dimension, trying to grasp the meaning of it all. It is the same old magic on a summer evening when the crowds and the banners are thick, or on a cold winter evening when the breath hangs heavy in the night air, and you have only a man and his dog for company. As the notes fade plaintively, this "great army" seems to hem you in, pleading for remembrance, and as you gaze at that awesome panorama of names carved in stone you want to believe that the 40,000 men buried around this little town can actually hear this nightly tribute to their sacrifice.

A visit to the Menin Gate at evening time is an experience with no equal. It is as if the Creator himself has touched this place with love and peace.

Perhaps some of us do tend to grieve and remember too much until it controls a large part of our lives, but if the collective sacrifice of these men did anything, it gave us the freedom to remember them in our individual ways.

Ypres has become synonymous with sacrifice, duty and suffering, but that is not to say every man who breathed his tortured last in the mud af Passchendaele or elsewhere gave thanks to King and country. They did not, and we would be foolish to think otherwise. It was probably thoughts of home and loved ones that occupied their last moments. So what is left to us in this small corner of Belgium but to remember them with pride and affection, and the people of Ypres with their eloquent tribute each evening at the Menin Gate gives us such an opportunity. That is the abiding memory of Ypres.

No book of this kind can get lift-off without the help and support of others. Its pages are dedicated unreservedly to Lyn Macdonald who suggested *Salient Points* to me while on a trip to Flanders. Lyn has always offered great encouragement and support, and also kindly allowed me to quote from one of her books *The Roses of No Man's Land* (Michael Joseph, 1980).

I am indebted to Paul Reed for his help in keeping me on the track factually. There is no doubt that Paul, despite his youth, is one of the keenest brains on the Great War in Britain today.

Before he died in 1991 this work found favour with John Giles, founder of the Western Front Association, and it gave me great pleasure that John pushed me to complete it. He was always a friend and mentor from the publication of his own successful *Ypres Salient, Then and Now,* (Leo Cooper, 1974).

Thanks are accorded to the Commonwealth War Graves Commission for their general assistance and approval to reprint detail of several cemeteries under their control in Flanders.

My sincere thanks go to Jonathan Nicholls, author of the book on Arras (1917) *The Cheerful Sacrifice* (Leo Cooper, 1990) for his introduction to *Salient Points*, and further thanks to Jim Ludden who applied his creative talent to the front cover.

I am grateful to Mrs Peggy Crowle for permission to repeat the story of her late father Sergeant Harry Combes, DCM, RGA, which appeared in *The Anatomy of a Raid* (Multidream, 1991), and to Gordon Davidson for allowing the story of his uncle, Captain Ronald Davidson, Royal Scots, to appear in these pages.

I would like to thank Tonie and Valmai Holt who have been supportive throughout, and their book on Bruce Bairnsfather, *In Search of a Better 'Ole* (Milestone Publlications, 1985) helped in compiling the Cameo on 'Old Bill'.

Ted Smith has been his usual tower of strength not only with his editing, checking and research but his continued support which has allowed this book to see the light of day. If it has any merit in its design and general presentation, then it is the general input of Ted Smith which has been the major influence.

A.Spagnoly, 1993.

PREFACE

Ypres! The very name is like a sledgehammer to the emotions. It is difficult to convey the significance of the name to the British Army. Ypres was a symbol to an island racey. A name drawn in blood and suffering, emphasizing the determination and tenacity of a people unwilling to yield, and to shrug off any perception of defeat. From the earliest days of the Great War until October 1918 when, from the untold thousands aimed at the little town, the last shells fell into the Grande Place, nearly every British division serving on the Western Front experienced the hell that was the Ypres Salient and would record a part of it on its Battle Honours. Speak the names quietly of the little hamlets and emotive spots which ringed the town to form that dreaded Salient: Hooge; Hill 60; Zillebeke; St Eloi; Zonnebeke; St Julien; Langemarck amongst others and, the most terrible of all ... Passchendaele! How these names will recall those brutal and dreadful days to many.

Before the guns fell silent in November 1918 over 2,000 men lay buried within the confines of Ypres, with thousands more outside the ramparts, in resting places or commemorated on the many memorials to the missing.

From the beginning to the end of the war, Ypres would never be more than seven miles from the front line, subjected to all the daily pressure and terrors that a professional Teutonic Order could inflict. Even in the darkest days of Spring 1918, the line forming the Salient bent, strained and stretched taut ... but to break and fall to admit the enemy hordes ... never.

So to the traveller of today, reflect, because yours is a pilgrimage in memory of those that have passed this way. You should tread with reverence, because this will forever be sacred ground. It is a shrine for all of those that have gone before. Today you can walk in peace where once it meant certain death. Those times may seem distanced from our more sophisticated age but the debt we owe them down the years is eternal. Their sacrifice can never be erased.

For this is the Immortal Salient

A. Spagnoly, 1993.

INTRODUCTION

In November this year, it will be 75 years since the Great War of 1914–18 ended and the last gun boomed out in anger across the tortured wastes of the Western Front. Soon we shall be entering the 21st Century and the generation of young men who fought in that great British Army of 1914-18 will have gone for ever. With their passing will go the memories of the Ypres Salient, the defence of which cost Britain and her Empire upwards of 400,000 of its best men and was probably the greatest demonstration of human endurance and sacrifice that Britain contributed towards the history of the 20th Century.

Today we seem to live in an age gone mad. Crime is rife and, above all, juvenile crime is continually the focus of media attention. Yet all is not lost. In March this year I attended the Mobbs Memorial Match at Northampton Rugby Club. This annual game of Rugby football commemorates the life of one of my heroes, Edgar Mobbs, Captain of Saints and England. He was killed in action in the Ypres Salient at some forgotten place called Lower Star Post on 31 July 1917, whilst commanding the 7th Battalion, Northamptonshire Regiment.

This annual game of rugby football was attended by thousands of enthusiastic youngsters who for a brief period of their education were given the opportunity to remember a very great man. Edgar Mobbs is hopefully a source of inspiration for future generations of Northamptonshire school children. As Winston Churchill wrote; "The future is uncertain but the past should give us hope."

Today's National Curriculum for Schools includes compulsory learning about the history and origins of the Great War of 1914-18 and it is no bad thing. Together with Alf Razzel, a well known veteran soldier of that terrible conflict, I have recently been speaking to many local schools on that very topic. For a 96-year-old who fought in the Ypres Salient of 1915, seeing the fresh wide-eyed faces of interested children has given Alf Razzel further zest for life. Many schools are nowadays visiting the old Western Front and, in particular, the Ypres Salient. It is to our teachers that we must turn to tell of the heroic achievements of a generation of young men that forged the Immortal Salient.

Hopefully our children will carry this torch of remembrance into the next century. From the current generation they will inherit a great wealth of literature about the Great War of 1914-18. Some books will teach them well. *Salient Points* is such a book.

Dozens of books have been written about the Ypres Salient and they keep coming. This book is different. It is a collection of short, colourful pen-pictures about almost forgotten episodes in the life of the Salient, through which runs a distinct thread of love for the characters and places that are so accurately brought to life by Tony Spagnoly and Ted Smith.

Since the passing of Rose Coombs and John Giles, there are few people left among us who possess that special knowledge of the Ypres Salient. Tony Spagnoly is one such person. In the rebuilt villages, woods and fields that were the Ypres Salient, the ghosts of a great armies dwell. *Salient Points* is a fine companion for any visitor to these secret places. Enjoy it and remember with pride.

Jonathan Nicholls, May 1993.

Photograph : Ted Smith

Larch Wood (Railway Cutting) Cemetery as seen from the old British front line at the foot of Hill 60, just behind what was Trench 39. Visible in the background are the spires of the Cloth Hall and St. Martin's Cathedral, Ypres. The slight rise in the ground outside the walls of the cemetery just in front of the Cross of Sacrifice identifies the workings of the Berlin Sap which served as the entrance to the tunnel used to lay the charges under Hill 60 and the Caterpillar. Slightly off the beaten track, Larch Wood is not one of the more frequently visited of the military cemeteries and it is difficult to imagine that this was the last comparatively safe spot on the way from Ypres to Hill 60.

XIV

To this new concert, white we stood,
Cold certainty held our breath;
While men in the tunnels below Larch Wood
Were kicking men to death.
From *Concert Party, Busseboom,* by Edmund Blunden.

1

LARCH WOOD (RAILWAY CUTTING) CEMETERY
Hill 60, Zillebeke, Ypres, 1915-1917

HILL 60 IS A NAME SYNONYMOUS with slaughter on the most vicious scale within the restricted confines of the Ypres Salient, and possibly the whole of the British Western Front during the Great War. At first sight it belies the evil name and reputation it acquired within the context of that war. It is a small insignificant rise of spoil made from the digging of the Ypres-to-Menin railway cutting which runs alongside it. Rising only sixty metres above sea level, hence the name given to it by army cartographers, it proved to be of great tactical importance during the military operations conducted in the area during the years 1915–17. The land contours surrounding it are generally flat and because of this the isolated hillock became of paramount importance due to the view it commanded over the village of Zillebeke and its famous lake, and almost over to the gates of Ypres itself. That age old maxim, 'In the land of the blind, the one-eyed man is King", was never better applied than at Hill 60.

Details of the many battles and mining operations that flowed over and under these infamous slopes are duly recorded in a host of military books and histories written over the years. Suffice to say that, from the conception of the Messines offensive in 1915, culminating in its opening battle on 7th June 1917 with the blowing of the Hill 60 mine and its twin in the neighbouring Caterpillar position, the Hill and its intricate system of trench lines around its' base were never quiet, though quite static. Hill 60 became a by-word for savagery as each side fought desperately to deprive the other of its advantage.

Visitors to the Western Front from wherever they come have made the pilgrimage and paid due honour to the countless young men who fell there. Thankfully it was purchased for the British nation to remain part of its military heritage for all time, with the many memorials in the area maintained by the Commonwealth War Graves Commission and its dutiful staff in Ypres. Visitors and pilgrims have experienced the imposing silence and all-pervading melancholy sadness which somehow charges the air at this strangely noble place. They have stood in respectful meditation alone with their thoughts on these brooding slopes and silently contemplated the many memorials, mine-craters and ruined pill-boxes. Some of the more sensitive will have felt the vibrations or echoes of long ago moving silently and sadly over the neat sheep-cropped grass like wraiths from the past, not quite comprehending the awesome power of it all.

Hill 60 allegedly holds the remains of several thousands of men from both sides who died in the brutal fighting during the years 1915-17. In June 1917 alone, when the mine exploded beneath it at the opening of the Messines offensive, two German companies of the resident garrison were lost and approximately 600 young souls were consigned to eternity in a split second.

Looking to Ypres from the bridge leading across the railway to the hamlet of Verbrandenmolen, a small military burial plot can be seen nestling in the slope of the hill alongside the rail track. One of the earliest cemeteries constructed around Ypres after the Armistice, it is named Larch Wood (Railway Cutting) Cemetery after a plantation of larch trees which stood there in 1914. French troops holding the area carved dug-outs at the northern end to afford protection in the lee of the railway banks and sketches of the time show their openings in the trees, together with wooden crosses marking the graves of the earliest French casualties, since removed to the French cemetery at Potijze.

When the British army moved into this sector to relieve the French in late 1914, they consolidated and built on what was already in existence. As the trench-lines became fixed and the fighting on and around the hill intensified, the sheltered position of Larch Wood gave it an importance that the troops were thankful for, and glad to exploit. Dug-outs and trenches were scooped out and deepened in and around the cutting and communication trenches were dug from the plantation, winding up the tortuous slope to the menace of Hill 60 itself, allowing a steady flow of men and materials to enter the front line in comparative safety. The main communications trench, numbered 38, ran its course like an artery feeding troops into trenches 37 and 39 at the very base of the hill along where the road runs today.[1]

Every night from the direction of Ypres parties of weary men, taking advantage of a darkness interrupted only by the spluttering relief of the odd Verey light, collected ammunition, food, wire and other trench materials from the pioneer dumps around Zillebeke Lake, Transport Farm and Transport Dug-outs. Then they would slog along the safer side of the railway embankment, named Lover's Lane by army cartographers not completely devoid of humour,

3

to drop their loads at Larch Wood Tunnels as the area came to be known. On their return to Ypres and Zillebeke, they would escort the walking wounded back to the main dressing stations near Ypres, the largest of these being Railway Dug-outs (Transport Farm) on the edge of the village of Zillebeke itself.

Those who were killed at Hill 60 or Larch Wood, or who died of wounds there, were buried in what is now Larch Wood (Railway Cutting) Cemetery, a plot enlarged to over 800 graves after 1918 when the surrounding area was cleared of the dead.[2] These men had been treated at the large aid station specially set up at Larch Wood Tunnels to cope with the ever increasing number of casualties filtering down from the hill.

During the summer of 1916 the British were implementing their plan for an offensive on the Messines Ridge the following year, laying twenty-five mines to set off the attack. In the event, one was lost through enemy action and one was discovered by the Germans near Messines and abandoned after being flooded from the waters of the River Douve. A slab of concrete in the yard of La Petite Douve Farm today covers the shaft dug by the Germans to investigate the workings of this mine. Only nineteen mines were blown on the day of the attack. One of the remaining four exploded in 1955, much to the surprise and concern of the local community, and the other three are still in place. One is the twin of that which exploded in 1955 and is believed to be on the other side of the road to Warneton from where that explosion occurred. The other two are referred to by the Australian historian Dr. C. E. W. Bean in one of his volumes covering Australian activity in the war – but that is another story.

A mineshaft, the Berlin Sap, had been sunk just east of Larch Wood Tunnels serving as the entrance to the tunnel used to lay charges of ammonal under Hill 60 and, through a tributary of the main tunnel, the Caterpillar, its twin defensive position just across the railway on the western edge of a light woodland known as Battle Wood. The mines were exploded in June 1917 and all objectives achieved, although a counter-mining break into the Berlin Tunnel by the Germans at the junction leading to the Caterpillar was only repaired and the mine under the Caterpillar primed a few hours before zero hour. The resulting craters can be seen today although the Caterpillar is full of water and lies in private ground.[3] The small grassy mound close to the railway just east of the cemetery wall is the site of the original workings of the Berlin Sap. This quiet, gentle spot is all that remains of a noisy workplace so well known by those tunnellers of many years ago.

Captain John Eden of the 12th Lancers, killed in action on 17th October 1914 between the village of Zillebeke and the Menin Road whilst on patrol with his squadron, lies in Larch Wood. He was the elder brother of Sir Anthony Eden, Earl of Avon, the British Foreign Secretary during the Munich crisis in 1938, Prime Minister in 1953, later resigning after the Anglo-French attack on the Suez Canal in 1956. Sir Anthony served in the Ypres Salient in the summer of 1917 with the 21st Battalion King's Royal Rifle Corps, 41st Division, and was involved in operations near Raven Wood, St. Eloi, not too far from Larch Wood. However, in his memoirs covering the period he never mentions having visited his brother's grave, although he refers to him several times with great affection.

The cemetery, a tranquil spot to sit and meditate, is well worth a visit. To reach it cross the railway bridge at Hill 60 and turn right into the road leading to Shrapnel Corner and Ypres.[4] On the right hand side about 200 yards along this road the familiar sign of the Commonwealth War Graves Commission points along a little farm-track leading across the railway line to the cemetery. Apart from the natural growths of trees and grasslands and the modern buildings and industrial units creeping up the far skyline from Zillebeke village, today's view from Larch Wood towards Hill 60 has not altered unduly, but it is still a battle with the emotions to reconcile that this scene of peace and tranquillity today could have been a place of such devastation and suffering in a not too distant past.[5]

The farming community of Zillebeke who planted and nurtured this plantation of larch trees in the early years of the century could have had no conception of what it would mean to men from foreign lands during a forthcoming war, nor of its permanent *raison d'être* after the conflict.

Its position besides the Ypres-to-Menin railway bank in the protective lee of an innocent hillock comprising a sixty-metre-high pile of spoil, dug out to allow passage for the railway, caused it, and the hillock, to enter forever the military annals of three war-stricken nations: first the French, then their old enemy the British and, pitted against both, the Germans. What was originally intended as a source of wood became a dropping-off point for supplies, equipment and materials, a place of surveillance, a last stop in the communication line to the battle front, a place for engineers and miners to start a tunnel opening the way to the laying of two massive explosive charges under the

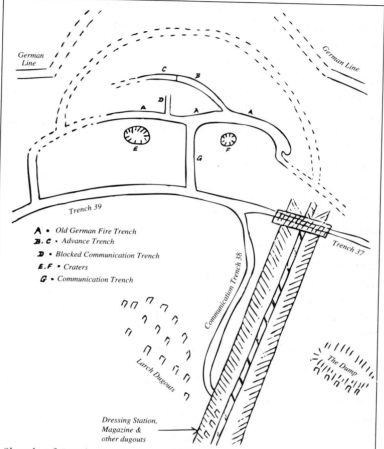

Sketch of Larch Dug-outs and Hill 60 by Leslie Yorath Sanders
reproduced from *A Soldier Of England*, (J. Maxwell & Son, 1920).

*"A and C companies then made their way to the line ... They occupied
'Larch Dug-outs' in the larch wood on the left of the cutting. It was
reported that C company lost six men by shell fire on the way. In these
dug-outs we lay all that day, through the night, and until nearly dark
the next day, being shelled continuosly, but not heavily, the whole
time."*

hillock and its sister across the railway track, and it was to become for many a place of shelter and caring and, sadly for others, a last resting place.

The plantation has long gone, its wartime activities and usage now only records in military history and occasional mentions in personal memoirs, but the railway bank is still there, the hillock is still there and many of the young men who waged war in the area are still there.

Notes :

1. Trench 38 was the main communication trench leading from Larch Wood up the slopes to Hill 60 itself. Trench 39 was the British front line trench which lay roughly along the line of the road running along the base of the hill today.

2. The cemetery records 856 Graves – 614 soldiers and airmen from the U.K.; 85 from Canada; 35 from Australia; 1 from the British West Indies Regiment; 33 whose units are not known; 1 Canadian merchant seaman; 321 unnamed graves, and memorials to 81 United Kingdom soldiers and 1 Australian. The remains of the French casualties originating the plot now rest at the French military cemetery, St. Charles, at Potijze.

3. The Caterpillar crater is in private ground. Permission to visit is needed, although a small track aside the railway-line leads into Battle Wood and the Caterpillar.

4. The French memorial at the railway bridge honours two French prisoners-of-war shot by the Germans in 1940 while trying to escape from a passing train. A Zillebeke local witnessed the killings as a young boy, giving a descriptive account of the drama in 1982 to John Giles, the Founder of the Western Front Association, on a visit to Hill 60.

5. Bullet-holes and slight damage seen on the Hill 60 memorials stem from skirmishing in May 1940 during World War II when British troops were defending the Comines canal. A museum in a café at the base of the hill, sited on the old trench line, was maintained by an Ypres veteran of the British Army until the late 1960s. A small museum still exists there, though not in any way linked to the original, but the British trench-lines have disappeared.

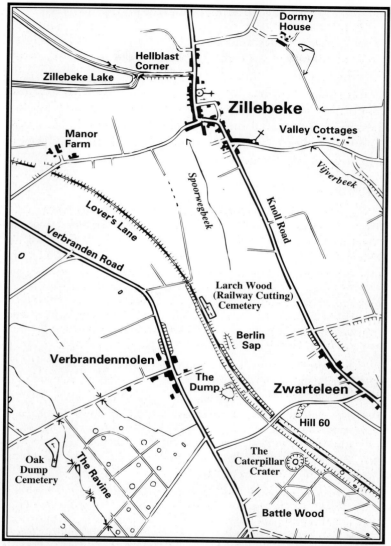

Larch Wood (Railway Cutting) Cemetery sits alongside the Ypres-to-Menin railway line with the small rise in the field in front showing the site of the Berlin Sap.

9

THOMAS KEITH HEDLEY RAE.

2

SECOND LIEUTENANT KEITH RAE
8th Rifle Brigade Private Memorial, Sanctuary Wood, Ypres

THOMAS KEITH HEDLEY RAE, known by friends and family as Keith, was born in Birkenhead on 24th May 1889 to a family of middle-class income. His early school years were plagued with bouts of ill-health and it was thought his constitution too frail to withstand the rigour of the spartan public school life to which he aspired. However, he insisted and persevered, finally winning through, gaining in 1907 a well merited scholarship to Balliol College, Oxford.

He was a hard-working student, eager to learn and, as he grew to be more robust in nature and physique, became more involved in sporting and outside activities. At Balliol he developed a friendship with Ronald Poulton Palmer of the prosperous Reading family known for their biscuit-making company, Huntley and Palmer.[1] Palmer, a rugby player of national repute, assisted Keith in helping deprived local youth to aspire to a better way of life. One of Keith's crowning achievements was to have founded and developed a flourishing boys' club in Oxford whose activities he closely monitored and which he helped to finance. The club survived him years after his death, and many a local lad who found a better path in life has reason to remember the name of Keith Rae with gratitude.

He was awarded his teaching diploma in 1913 and had

set himself a career as a tutor at Marlborough College, Wiltshire when the storm clouds broke out over Europe and, in the August of 1914, Great Britain declared war against Germany. Although he did not relish the thought of the hardships of life within the military and even flinched from the prospect, he did not allow these forebodings to hinder him in his perceived duty and, joining in the national euphoria of that period, volunteered for service with a host of fellow students from Oxford.

He was swiftly commissioned into the Rifle Brigade by virtue of a personal contact and found himself with the 8th Battalion of that regiment, at the time under training near Aldershot with the 14th (Light) Division, one of the New Army divisions. Training was completed without incident and, around the middle of May 1915, the formation was shipped out to France, landing at Le Havre and experiencing its first taste of France in camp at Watten close to the picturesque hill town of Cassel.[2]

The Division was then moved by units into the line around Ypres for general instruction and acclimatization in trench warfare. The 8th Battalion found itself at Railway Wood just east of Ypres and north of the Menin Road, a notoriously active sector of the British front. It would now spend the next month or so manning the trenches at Hooge, a small village cresting a rise on the Menin Road east of the wood. Their trenches were close to the château of a baronial estate in the village, Hooge Château, and here the Battalion was to experience a fierce baptism of fire and, in the process, learn many a hard and tragic lesson. Second Lieutenant Rae, who had proved himself to be an efficient and valuable platoon officer in C Company, would play a full and gallant part in these proceedings.

On 30th July 1915 at the tail-end of the Second Battle of Ypres a tragedy was to strike C Company. The area around Hooge was a sensitive salient jutting into the British line along the Menin Road. It had recently been captured from a stunned enemy after the blowing of a massive mine under its defences. The mine had been tunnelled-in from Tunnel House, a farm complex laying about 100 metres south of the Menin Road directly opposite the Château itself.[3] The Germans responsible for this sector soon recovered from this hammer blow and, as expected, their considered and immediate response was not long in coming, being launched in the early hours of the 30th July. Second Lieutenant Rae and his platoon were part of the duty garrison manning the fire-trench leading off from the right of the crater towards the Château stables, so recently and bloodily fought over and now completely destroyed.[4] It was an attack of massive proportion, with the Germans intent on winning back their foothold on this strategically valuable position which afforded such good observation.

A violent barrage preceded a flood of enemy storm-troops carrying a new and fearsome weapon being used for the first time. Liquid fire jetting from canisters strapped to the backs of specially selected and trained men brought a new and terrifying dimension of attack to the luckless defenders who had no chance of withstanding it. Though gallantly resisting, the British line began to break as men of the Rifle Brigade and King's Royal Rifle Corps were forced away from the crater and out of the Château grounds to withdraw in confusion to the south of the Menin Road where, badly shaken by the devastating effects of the new weapon, they mustered and reformed. Survivors of the action spoke of Second Lieutenant Rae at the height of the fighting standing on the parapet badly burned and bleeding, firing his revolver at the approaching enemy with only his platoon sergeant for company. It was said : "He was splendidly regardless of his life and fighting against fearful odds." He was never seen again.

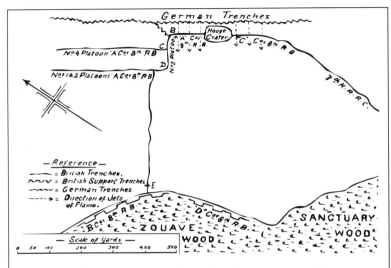

The German "Liquid Fire" attack on the 8th Battalion and the counter-attack by the 7th and 9th Battalions from Zouave Wood, 31st July 1915. Reproduced from *The Rifle Brigade 1914–1918, Volume I* by Reginald Berkeley, (Butler & Tanner Ltd., 1927).

From Zouave Wood, a small plantation on the edge of Sanctuary Wood, the depleted force immediately mounted a counter-attack in an attempt to retrieve the crater position. It proved to be an abject failure with the Riflemen labouring up the hostile slope facing point-blank fire and, adding insult to injury, being held back by their own wire which had been quickly utilized by a triumphant enemy.[5]

When the area was searched for the fallen after the

hostilities, Second Lieutenant Rae's body was never recovered.[6] This was no surprise in view of the grim pounding this area took over the three years following, with the Hooge Château and its crater being almost the fulcrum of the Ypres Salient during this period. His name is commemorated on the Menin Gate Memorial at Ypres together with that of a fellow officer, Second Lieutenant Sydney Woodroffe who died in the action. Woodroffe was to receive a posthumous Victoria Cross, one of the first awarded to a member of the New Army.

A Celtic cross memorial was erected by the Rae family in the grounds of Hooge Château near the site where he was last seen. In 1968, however, at the request of the late Baron de Vinck who owned the estate, it was removed to Sanctuary Wood Military Cemetery where it stands today on the grass verge just outside the gate of the cemetery.

The memorial to the 14th (Light) Division stood deep within the leafy glades of Railway Wood and was a much visited place of pilgrimage and remembrance. With the passing of time the ground beneath began to subside due to the numerous mine-workings and tunnels below, thereby weakening its foundations. It was thought prudent that a better site be found for it and, under the auspices of Colonel John Baker, Rifle Brigade, and thanks to the efforts of the Green Jackets depôt at Winchester, working with a team of young British soldiers stationed in Germany, it was dismantled and re-erected beside the Hill 60 Memorial in the commune of Zillebeke, where it can be seen today.

Notes :

1. Lieutenant Ronald Poulton Palmer, 1/4th Berks, was rugby captain for his county and England, last playing for England against France at Parc des Princes, in July 1914. His final game was as captain of a 48th Div.

team beating a 4th Div. team 17–0 at Pont de Nieppe on April 14th 1915. He was killed on May 5th 1915 while in charge of a working party in the line at Anton Farm near Ploegsteert Wood. He was buried on the evening of the 6th by the Bishop of Pretoria in the Battalion cemetery on the eastern edge of the wood. England still play France in an annual Police rugby fixture competing for the Ronald Poulton Palmer Cup.

2. The historical town of Cassel, perched on a hill of the same name, was visited by Field Marshal Foch, Sir Douglas Haig and His Majesty King George V. The hill is that in the ditty referring to the Marlborough campaign well known by generations of children who have sung : *The grand old Duke of York, he had ten thousand men, he marched them up to the top of the hill and he marched them down again.*

3. Tunnel House, from which the tunnel was worked for the mine causing the Hooge crater, was destroyed and never rebuilt.

4. Some visitors mistakenly assume that Hooge Crater cemetery is the site of the crater itself. The crater, now an ornamental pond inside the gates of what is today called Hooge Château, is on the other side of the Menin Road. Pill-boxes on its edge pose questions as to what sort of ornamentation it deserves.

5. Zouave Wood was cleared after the war and was never replanted.

6. A casualty of the counter-attack from Zouave Wood was Billy Grenfell, brother of poet Julian. His body was never found. He is commemorated on the Menin Gate at Ypres. He was killed within half a mile of where Julian had been wounded. Julian, a poet serving with the cavalry, died in a hospital in Boulogne from a wound received near Railway Wood during Second Ypres. He lies in the Boulogne Eastern British Military Cemetery. A cousin, Francis, awarded the V.C. at Mons in 1914, was killed at virtually the same spot where Julian was wounded. Buried at Vlamertinghe British Military Cemetery, he was one of the first officers to be awarded the V.C. in the Great War. A fourth cousin, Riversdale, was killed on the Aisne heights in September 1914 and is buried at Vendresse on the Chemin des Dames near Soissons. Another member of this redoubtable family, Joyce Grenfell the actress and comedienne, died in the 1980's having lived most of her life near Taplow Court, the family home in Berkshire. Taplow Court, the home of Lord and Lady Desborough, the parents of Julian and Billy, was used as a hospital for the Canadians in World War II.

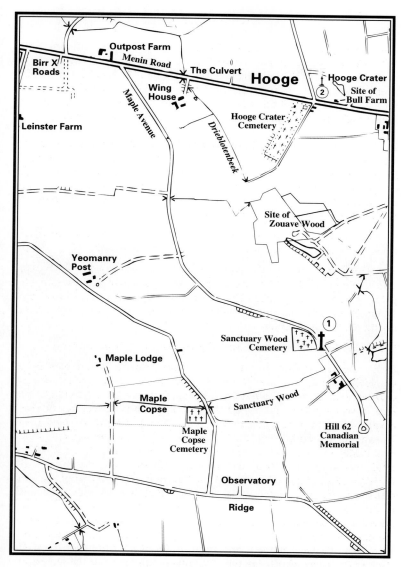

1. The Memorial to Keith Rae just outside Sanctuary Wood cemetery.
2. The original site of the Memorial to Keith Rae in Château Wood.

17

Photograph : Ted Smith

Bellewaarde Farm and the line of sawn-down tree trunks which marked the old German front trench line. The Germans used wooden piquets in the early stages of the war and from these grew this line of trees. The farmer has since ripped-out these stumps but the state of the land in the fields surrounding the farm still gives a clear indication of the fire and communication trenches that once dominated this area.

18

In lonely watches night by night
Great visions burst upon my sight,
For down the stretches of the sky
The hosts of dead go marching by.
From *Requiescant* by Frederick George Scott.

3

BELLEWAARDE FARM
Hooge Ridge, Zillebeke Commune, Ypres, 1915-1918

TRAVELLING FROM THE TOWN of Ypres along the Menin Road at the crossroads just before the gradual rise of the Hooge ridge there lies the infamous Hell Fire Corner. It is worth pausing a while at this notorious corner to ponder a place that belies its evil past.[1]

Here during the Great War men would hunch forward in dreaded anticipation, and agitated drivers and limber teams would speed up somewhat before their presence or betraying dust-patterns alerted the ever watchful enemy observers on the high ground just ahead. Long strips of hessian material erected at the side of the road to cover any movement did not always do the trick and accurate German gunfire zeroed on the crossroads could herald death and destruction at any time of day and night. The vacant, shuttered estaminet that stood here for so many post-war years lent an air of genteel dereliction to the corner, like an aged lady who had known better days. The Invader Stone, taking pride of place in its position at the centre of the junction, glints in the weak Flemish sun as a danger of another kind marks the spot today – traffic speeding in both directions, to or away from Ypres itself.[2] The place seems to sigh for another time, more dangerous but nobler perhaps amidst the pace of modern living.

Bearing supplies, sweating men with terrified horses

would load or unload small-arms ammunition and other front line materials at Rifle Farm, a large rural holding rebuilt today on its old site just beyond the corner.[3] Walking wounded who had limped into the advanced aid posts at Birr Cross Roads[4] would be escorted past the corner back to the regimental aid stations around Ypres, the more seriously wounded being transported to the casualty clearing stations towards Poperinghe where more sophisticated treatment was available before they were transported to the French coast and, for the luckier ones, on to "Blighty", for hospitalization.

Throughout the years of conflict when the British fought at such great cost to stay the hands of the enemy around Ypres, countless men slogged up the Menin Road from the ramparts of the town and on past Hell Fire Corner. Once past they would filter gratefully into the fields on either side of the shell-battered and historic highway, moving forward to man the trench-lines around Railway Wood, Sanctuary Wood and the very fulcrum of the Salient itself, the village of Hooge sitting atop its all-important rise on the Menin Road to the east of Ypres. This strategically placed little hamlet vied in importance with Hill 60 slightly to the south as a place where combat of the fiercest intensity took place.

On the left of the Menin Road just north of Birr Cross Roads the mass of Railway Wood[5] hugged the slope and sentries manning the trenches and saps edging it would stare across No Man's Land to the ruins of Bellewaarde Farm, lying snug and safe in its hollow just behind the German front trenches. The line was pretty static at this spot during the period from the close of Second Ypres in May 1915 until the opening of the Passchendaele offensive on the 31st July 1917, the start of Third Ypres. Units of the British 8th Division opened this battle with great success locally, advancing an unparalleled distance of 2,000 yards on the first day, leap-frogging all the enemy positions up to the Westhoek ridge.

In the intervening years, however, gaunt and bleary-eyed sentries from both sides would scour the ground between the lines near Bellewaarde Farm, ever watchful for activity or movement across the way. Regular and aggressive patrolling and trench raiding were major features of the war fought here and, as if that wasn't enough, active mining was prevalent on these slopes. Begun by the Germans, but improved upon and intensified by the British, the advantages continually swayed between the combatants. Both enjoyed good observation, that of the British from Railway Wood overlooking the flat meadows to the Ypres-Roulers railway embankment and the Frezenberg Ridge beyond, while the Germans commandeered views towards Sanctuary Wood, Zillebeke, Hill 60, and, more importantly, the Menin Road and the gates of Ypres itself.

The British, in their bid to unlock the enemy stranglehold around Ypres, frequently attempted to nudge the enemy off his prime location on the Hooge Ridge and several major operations were mounted over the years to meet this objective.[6] In June of 1915 the 1st Battalion Honourable Artillery Company tried to clear the slope at Y Wood and, in July 1915, the 3rd Division with the 14th (Light) Division were active at Hooge Château in an abortive counter-attack from Zouave Wood following the loss of Hooge when the Germans introduced their new weapon of liquid fire. More operations were initiated

21

around Railway Wood in September 1915 to assist the Loos battles further south, but all to no avail, and each time with a great loss of life.

An important ingredient in this German defensive work was machine-gun fire from dug-outs and trench-works skilfully built in and around the ruins of Bellewaarde Farm.[7] In comparative safety he was able to ensure the security of the area across the Hooge crest and the field of fire and wire defences helped him retain this commanding feature, threatening Ypres until the July 1917 battles.

Today when the visitor stands deep in thought between Railway Wood and the grave of men of the Royal Engineers[8] on the highest part of the ridge, he can view the passing traffic along the Menin Road, and inwardly gasp at the strength of this enemy sector and perhaps smile ruefully at the Flemish cattle now grazing in what was No Man's Land, watering with tranquil ease at one of the bowl-like depressions which once erupted with all the fury that a mine explosion could muster. Until a few years ago many craters of varying sizes were to be found, testifying to the intense mine warfare waged hereabouts. Local farmers have gradually filled them, leaving just a few to collect water, affording some drinking availability for their cattle. The earth has still not settled following those eruptions and it is easy to locate the main crater positions close to the Royal Engineers' grave, isolated but standing proud, commemorating the work of the tunnelling companies and their special brand of warfare conducted below the earth.

Behind the grave the ground is a deep impenetrable mass of foliage, jumbled craters and trench-lines extending back to Bellewaarde Farm itself, one of the few areas of the Western Front deemed impossible to cultivate, an abiding testimonial from those desperate days. The turbulent nature of this tortured earth is strangely impressive. A side-track leads past the farm across the Bellewaarde Beke, just where an arm of Y Wood existed, meeting the Menin Road at the little chapel of Hooge where each November a nameless person leaves a plain cross for a veteran in memory of someone long gone at this place. It is a rewarding experience to walk this track.

Looking from the Royal Engineers' grave to the Menin Road, Hell Fire Corner, Rifle Farm and Ypres, the panorama unfolds itself like no other on the northern part of the Western Front. From Bellewaarde Farm, hull down and safe in its defensive fold in the ground, it is easy to see how the Germans held sway over this stretch of No Man's Land for so long. From the farm, out into the meadow almost as far as the track that leads to Westhoek, a line of trees once lined the course of what was part of the German front trench-line. According to the late Mr. J. Higgins, a veteran of the Machine Gun Corps, who conducted British Legion battlefield tours in the 1920s and early 1930s, they grew from the wooden piquets placed along this stretch by the Germans and followed the course of their front line as indicated on sector maps of the time.

Notes :
1. The Ypres-Roulers railway crossed the Menin Road within yards of Hell Fire Corner and German artillery had the crossing accurately gauged. Effective fire could be, and was, brought to bear here at all times of the day and night.

2. Few Invader Stones remain today. Erected by the Touring Club de Belgique in the 1920s circling Ypres to mark the limit of the German attempts to capture it, the one at Hell Fire Corner was moved to its mid-road position by local authorities in an area improvement scheme.

3. Rifle Farm, on the Menin Road just beyond Hell Fire Corner toward Menin, was a dropping-off and collecting point for supplies.

4. Birr Cross Roads, named by the Leinster Regiment after their home depôt, housed an Aid Station and the size of today's military cemetery there testifies to its importance. A military road was started here in 1917 for men and materials to move in safer conditions towards the Westhoek Ridge via Château Wood.

5. Railway Wood, on the Hooge Ridge near the Ypres-Roulers railway line, named by army cartographers in 1914 for obvious reasons, saw fierce fighting for several years becoming a 14th (Light) Division's battle honour after their July 1915 attempt to hold Hooge after the German liquid fire attack. A divisional memorial stood in the wood until 1978 when an army team moved it to Hill 60 due to its foundations breaking up through earth subsidence. Captain A. O. Pollard V.C., in action here with the 1st Battalion Honourary Artillery Company in June 1915, records seeing German and British corpses "lying all over the place". In the German line he saw a dead Fusilier armed with an axe, its edge red with blood —"The Fusilier had reverted to the weapon of his forefathers".

6. The Royal Engineers' grave, bearing witness to the sacrifice of the men who fought underground, stands over the tunnels, now graves of three N.C.O.'s and eight other ranks who died below. The farmer at Bellewaarde, being concerned at the number of people visiting the grave and walking through his farm confines, prefers that those wishing to do so first ask for permission.

7. The line of trees marking the German line were sawn down in the 1980s. The stumps were used as electrified fence-posts until the early 90s when the farmer had them ripped-out – yet another trace of the Great War removed forever.

8. The Hooge and Bellewaarde Ridges are often confused. Hooge Ridge is the high ground on which stands the Royal Engineers' grave. The Bellewaarde Ridge is the bald dome of ground nestling at the foot of the rise to Westhoek Ridge at the far eastern end of the Bellewaarde Lake and Château Wood area where the Princess Pats of Canada fought their classic action in May 1915.

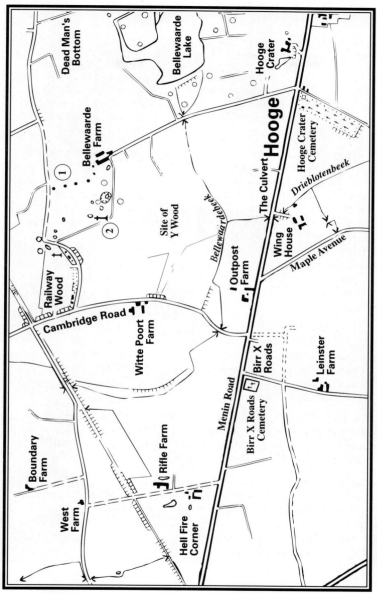

1. The line of trees that once marked the old German front line trench at Bellewaarde Farm

2. Royal Engineers Grave.

MAJOR WILLIAM REDMOND at the age of 54. (Feb. 1915)

"That quietly set, rather saddened face revealed the man possessed by an ideal; and all the forces of the world might beat for ever in vain against a resolve so great and stern."
T. P. O'Connor on Major Redmond.

4

MAJOR WILLIAM REDMOND
Irish Nationalist and Member of Parliament, Locre, Belgium

WILLIAM HOEY KEARNEY REDMOND, born in 1861 in Wexford, Ireland, was a man of wit and joyous intention, making no personal enemies even though caught up in the most partisan and bitter of political controversies as Ireland struggled to attain a measure of independence in the turbulent political activity of the period. The Redmonds were a prominent nationalist family and William must have reflected often on the statue in Redmond Place of his grand-uncle John Edward who in 1895 represented Wexford as the Liberal Member of Parliament. Before standing for Wexford himself in 1883, William was sent to Australia by William Parnell to raise funds for the nationalist cause, returning with the not inconsiderable sum for the time of fifteen thousand pounds. This expedition was successful for him in another way as he met and married Eleanor Dalton, daughter of an Australian judge. Redmond sat as Member of Parliament for Wexford until 1885 and his outspoken views on the political climate of the time led him into bitter conflict. He was sentenced to three months in prison for inciting resistance to arrest on a day of a local eviction. When led away he claimed : "I undoubtedly cheered those men when they were defending their homes against an unjust eviction – and I shall continue to cheer every man who does!"

27

Notwithstanding his views and utterances it was apparent that Redmond was a man of splendid purpose, the type of politician needed in the vortex of home rule that lay ahead. However, the black clouds of war were threatening Europe and, although well into his middle years, he left his home and career to train as a soldier, presuming perhaps that to taste combat would allow him a better platform to obtain a stronger hearing for Ireland at the London conference tables of the future. He also believed that Germany was the unjust aggressor and needed to be faced by all men good and true. A devout Catholic, foreseeing his own death, he willingly embraced the cause in the hope that his own sacrifice might bring healing to his troubled land. When he met his destiny in the summer of 1917 it caused such an expression of grief that his widow wrote : "If Willy could come back, he would be so surprised, he would wonder what all the fuss was about!"

At the age of fifty-six he was considered a little too old to chance the dangers of life in the trenches. Apart from that he was also viewed as a personage of some political importance and standing, but he meant to do his part and found himself in service at the front with the 6th Battalion Royal Irish Regiment, 16th (Irish) Division, then playing a prominent part in the Somme battles. This division was raised in the winter of 1914 by leading nationalists of the day, Hugh Devlin and John Redmond, the latter a relative of William. To don a British uniform was a moral dilemma of classic proportion, but his vision of the future had perceived the immediate fundamentals of the struggle and he warmed to the larger patriotism. On leaving for the war Redmond indicated : "If the Germans come here ... they will be our masters, and we at their mercy. What that mercy is likely to be, judge by the mercy shown to Belgium. I am far too old to be a soldier, but I mean to do my best, for whatever life remains in me ...".

He played a full part with his regiment as the division covered itself with glory at Ginchy and Guillemont in the 1916 Somme battles where a German officer declared : "We thought this position was impregnable – but they came at us like the devil. We could not withstand it."

Irish units taking serious losses saddened Redmond as he saw the potential of Irish blood being dissipated in the mud of the trenches. His health was suffering but, under friendly pressure to seek a way out, he would not leave his company. Having been seen by a comrade slumped over in his dug-out he finally succumbed and went home during 1916 to recuperate. On returning to France he was posted to divisional staff, which did not appeal to him.

Whilst alternating between the trenches and "Blighty" he made several appearances in the House and gave some fiery speeches. His final appearance was on the 7th March 1917 making a passionate plea for Home Rule in seconding T. P. O'Connor's motion for immediate implementation. This war-weary figure, speaking without any notes, held his audience spellbound. So absorbed was he in his theme that O'Connor, a leading Irish Nationalist, said afterwards that "men around him sobbed and wept unabashed". This was in fact his dying speech, a profession of faith, a testimony of all he had lived for, and what he was about to die for.

In June 1917 his destiny was almost upon him as the decision to explode the mines under the infamous enemy bastion, the Messines Ridge, went into its final planning stage. The 16th (Irish) Division at this time was located around the village of Locre close to Mount Kemmel, one of the most prominent features in Flanders. The divisional staff were housed in a convent near to the village church close to where a field hospital was established. The nuns in residence provided baths and hot food for the various units and it was here in the convent that Redmond entertained not only the Irish army chaplains but officers of the 36th (Ulster) Division. Men of this division were about to forge an undying link with their southern countrymen by attacking side-by-side with them for the first time in an attempt to capture the village of Wytschaete and the woodlands around it.[1]

Redmond was now a desperate man. His pleas to go "over-the-top" with his regiment had been refused by the commanding general. His fervour and persistence finally paid off when he was allowed to go, but only as far as the first objective. This was better than nothing and he prepared himself mentally and spiritually for the task ahead by partaking of Holy Communion with the nuns.

At 3.10 a.m. on the 7th June, 1917, nineteen mines erupted starting the Battle of Messines, blowing the many strong-points along the slopes of the ridge, together with their German defenders, into the heavens. The day was a success and casualties light, due in part to superb planning as Englishmen, Irishmen, Australians and New Zealanders rushed the stunned German positions and were on the reverse slope of the ridge within hours. Before the tortured earth had settled the Irish battalions were onto their objectives and had captured Petit Bois, Red Château, Unnamed Wood and the Hospice west of the village of Wytschaete which had seen the heaviest fighting of the day.[2] As the Royal Irish moved across the open meadow to their first objective, Petit Bois, Major Redmond was struck in the leg and then, almost immediately after, in the hand.[3] He fell as the advance flowed by and waited for attention, probably musing on his luck, as a condition of his being in the attack was that he would return to headquarters on reaching the first objective. He might have found it strange that it was stretcher-bearers from the 36th (Ulster) Division who attended to him before taking him to their dressing station and then to the 16th Field Ambulance on the Kemmel road. He received full consideration from these Ulstermen, in fact an English observer expressed surprise at the extreme care taken of the Major by those so politically opposed. Sadly, however, he was not destined to return alive. His wounds, although not serious, were too much for a constitution weakened by a long period of hardship in France and Flanders. Shock set in and he died before he could be moved to the convent at Locre.

When he did arrive there the grief of the nuns, who had formed a great attachment to him over the time he had been with them, was inconsolable. His body was laid out in the convent chapel where he had piously attended mass so often and, on the evening of the 8th June 1917, he was buried in the garden near the grotto to the Virgin Mary. One of his friends, an Irish chaplain, recorded : "No purer-hearted man, no braver soldier, ever died on the battlefield. He was absolutely convinced that he was dying for Ireland."

For many years after the war his grave was reverently tended by the nuns, but later, at the request of his family, his remains were exhumed and re-buried near the British military plot about 500 yards across the road from the

Hospice.[4] In a specific gesture, and as a mark of deep respect, Major Redmond was laid just outside the cemetery wall even though the British give complete equanimity in death to all their fallen. He lies there now, guarded for a while by sentry-like elm trees, since felled for reasons known only to the local farmer. It seems a fitting and most tranquil resting place for one who promised so much. The echoes of his loss are probably still felt in Ireland today.

Notes:

1. The attack on 7th June 1917 was one of the most successful days of the war for the allied troops. For the very first time Irishmen from the north and south, the 36th (Ulster) Division and the 16th (Irish) Division, fought side by side to sweep away all opposition and capture their allotted objectives. Several months later during the Passchendaele battles of August they were to fight together again on the Frezenberg Ridge near Zonnebeke, but this time with dire and tragic results. Rain, mud and a desperate defence by the Germans trapped the Irish units from both divisions in the waterlogged shallow bowl-like depressions of the battlefield and serious losses were inflicted on them.

2. Unnamed Wood was renamed Inniskilling Wood in honour of the Irishmen of 49th Brigade after the battles for Wytschaete in June 1917. The Hospice, so heavily fought over at the western fringe of the village, was never rebuilt, its site now being marked by the village tennis courts.

3. The area of ground on which Major Redmond received his wounds lies between the Petit Bois woodland and the mass of Grand Bois, Wytschaete 200 metres to the east. The two craters at Petit Bois are in open pastureland and are now full of water, used primarily by cattle to slake their thirst. A boring-machine, constructed from one used on the London Underground, was shipped to Belgium to assist in digging the tunnels to these craters. It was abandoned after consistently clogging in the Flemish mud and now lies eighty feet down near the craters, still waiting to be rescued. Vandamme Farm from which the workings of the tunnel to the Petit Bois mines started is still on its original site and distinguishable, due west of the craters, by its white walls and red roof.

4. Locre Hospice was badly damaged during the 1918 battles and was rebuilt a hundred metres or so away from its original site in the village.

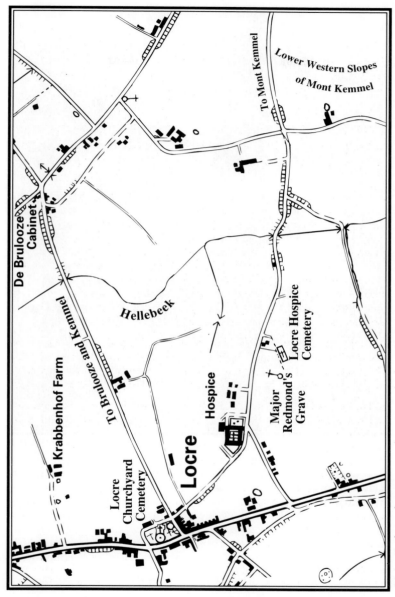

Major Redmond's grave sited just outside the Locre Hospice military cemetery opposite the Hospice itself.

Photograph : IWM Q3427

His Majesty King George V visiting the grave of Prince Maurice of Battenberg at the Ypres Town Cemetery soon after the Armistice. The King was one of the first members of the British Royal Family to visit the grave of Prince Maurice and did so when on a tour of the British military cemeteries on the Western Front just after the war. It was during this tour that King George expressed his desire that one of the larger pill-boxes captured at Tyne Cot near Passchendaele should be incorporated into the base of the cemetery's Cross of Sacrifice which would take its place in what is today Tyne Cot Military Cemetery.

34

So, soon they topped the hill and raced together
Over the open stretch of herbs and heather
Wilfrid Owen.

5

H. H. PRINCE MAURICE OF BATTENBERG
1st Battalion, K.R.R.C., Ypres Town Cemetery, Ypres

O N LEAVING THE TOWN of Ypres by the Menin Gate the
direction follows the footsteps of countless British
soldiers who trod this route to the front-line, many
thousands of whom never returned. If ever the British
army had a *Via Dolorosa* of its own, then this, the Menin
Road, is it. It traces the steps of legions of young men from
Britain and the Empire who trudged this shell-battered
route, hunched and tired, weary and laden, faces bared to
the relentless rain and the shell-swept skyline silhouetting
the village of Hooge perched on top of a slight rise on this
road east of Ypres. They would stagger and stumble their
way towards the trenches, usually in the dark to avoid
enemy observation on the high ground ahead, assisted
only by the blinding flash from a bursting shell or the
stuttering flare from a Verey light as it traced its route into
the night sky only to fall back to earth, spent and lifeless,
in moments.

A couple of hundred metres from the Menin Gate, the
battered opening in the Vauban ramparts that led the way
to Menin, the road forks and, whichever route they were
destined to take, the groups of respective infantrymen
knew of the pitfalls and dangers they were about to face
and had to overcome. They knew their chances were high
of not coming back at all, or of being badly enough hit to

spend a long period at a base hospital or in one back in "Blighty". The road forking to the right, the Menin Road itself, led to Hell Fire Corner and further up ahead, with the trench-lines hugging its surroundings, the village of Hooge, the very tip of the Ypres Salient from May 1915 to July 1917. This was a terrible spot in which to do one's duty in the line, and not for nothing did a wartime poet term the Menin Road *The Red Red Road to Hooge.*

The road forking left led to Frezenberg, Zonnebeke and Passchendaele, the latter a name that has gone down in military history as synonymous with death, destruction and suffering on a scale never before encountered in warfare. Along this road, within yards to the immediate right, is the Ypres Town Cemetery and Extension, developed in 1920 when the work of reconstruction commenced from the many local and battlefield graves that covered the region.[1] Thanks to the kindness of the town authorities the military graves were allotted an area alongside the communal civilian plot. This practice has been exercised in many towns and villages in this part of Belgium, illustrating poignantly the respect and thanks accorded by the local populace to the fallen sons of their British friends.

At the far end of the military section of the cemetery an opening leads to the civilian plots. Standing apart and isolated from the others, one particular grave just outside the walls of the military plot is notable for its military styling within a civilian type surround. This is the last resting place of one of the only members of the British Royal Household to fall in the Great War. It is that of His Highness Prince Maurice of Battenberg who fell in action on the 27th October 1914 during the opening phase of the First Battle of Ypres. At the time of his death Prince

Maurice was serving as a Lieutenant with the 1st Battalion King's Royal Rifle Corps, a part of the 2nd Division. The division at this period formed part of Sir Douglas Haig's I Corps and it had already seen action around the Belgian town of Mons in August of that year. History shows that this action was broken off quickly, and units of the corps would have a major role to play in the famous retreat that took them almost to the gates of Paris. The 1st Battalion King's Royal Rifle Corps, with Prince Maurice in its ranks, was engaged in all this activity, mostly acting in the role of a fighting rearguard to the retreating troops.

The Battalion arrived in Ypres on the night of October 20th and spent the next few days acting as support in the various actions taking place during this frenzied period, eventually moving through Zonnebeke to mount an attack towards the Keiburg Spur. This proved to be the Prince's last action which was recorded as :

On the 27th October 1914, the 1st British Corps commanded by Sir Douglas Haig was deployed in various defensive positions north and south of the Menin Road flexing itself to intervene and impede the advance of a mighty enemy force flooding in from due east (Menin) in a major bid to capture the town of Ypres and destroy the vastly outnumbered British Expeditionary Force in the process. With the British 7th Division already in position to withstand the onslaught abreast of the tragic highway, the 1st and 2nd Divisions would get their units out in front and form a covering screen north and south of the Menin Road to assist in blunting the enemy attack to which he attached very high hopes.

In an effort to forestall the enemy probes now beginning to spell danger, the Brigade (6th) to which the 1st K.R.R.C. belonged, struck out towards the east from the high ridge that ran from Broodseinde in the north to Becelaere in the south in the general direction of the Keiburg Spur approximately a mile distant, where German infantry had been observed. Marching through Zonnebeke, the riflemen crossed the highest section of the ridge at the Broodseinde crossroads and headed out into open and quite featureless country – and now themselves in full view of the advancing enemy. As they proceeded across country in open order their progress took them down a shallow valley and across a minor stream which lay across their front. As soon as they put the "beke" behind them, and began the slow tortuous ascent upwards towards the Spur and the little hamlet of Keiburg that gave its name to the general area – the enemy opened fire with small arms and light ordnance. Prince Maurice was hit by shrapnel from a shellburst very early on and was seen to fall to the ground. Although his platoon sergeant tried to administer assistance to the stricken Prince, he was found to be beyond any practicable help and died before his men could get him back to a temporary Advance Dressing Station at Zonnebeke.[2]

Prince Maurice was hit almost immediately the advance commenced, leading his men across the road atop the Broodseinde Ridge. As befitted his Royal rank, his body was taken to Ypres for burial. A military cemetery had been started alongside the civilian plot and, on 31st October 1914, he was laid to rest between the two under a temporary marker and cross. The cross remained there until 1921 when a more permanent headstone was erected and the grave was left in its isolated position where it is to be found today.

His Highness Prince Maurice Victor Donald of Battenberg K.C.V.O. was twenty-three years of age when he fell in action. He was the son of Henry Maurice of Battenberg and Princess Beatrice, the ninth child and youngest daughter of Queen Victoria. It was reputed that Her Majesty was very fond of the Prince and a charming photograph exists showing Her Majesty waiting calmly for the arrival of a visiting dignitary at Victoria Station with her grandson, the young Prince Maurice, standing dutifully at her side. The Prince was a direct cousin of the late Lord Louis Mountbatten whose father, Albert Battenberg, uncle of Prince Maurice, felt it necessary to resign as First Sea Lord at the Admiralty and change the family name to Mountbatten in the virulent anti-German atmosphere prevalent in 1914. At the time of Prince Maurice's death a close cousin and friend, Prince Albert of Schleswig-Holstein, was serving with the German army on another front. He was to survive the war.

The sister of Prince Maurice, Victoria Eugénie (Ena), consort and later widow of King Alphonso XIII of Spain, regularly travelled to Belgium to visit his grave until her own death in 1969. She was keen to have erected a special memorial to stand over the resting place of her beloved brother and approached the Prince of Wales in his capacity as President of the then Imperial War Graves Commission with her request. The Prince of Wales laid the matter before the King who refused to give his sanction. The King pointed out that it had been decided that the graves of all men who served and fell in the Great War, from generals to privates, were equal in honour and duty well and nobly done, and therefore should be marked by the same simple headstones. He wished no exception to be made in the case of a member of his own family.

King George V was one of the first members of the Royal Family to visit the grave when on a tour of the British war cemeteries soon after the Armistice. This was the visit when he expressed his desire that one of the larger pill-boxes captured at Tyne Cot near Passchendaele be incorporated into the base of the cemetery's Cross of Sacrifice to take its place in Tyne Cot Military Cemetery.

Queen Elizabeth II also paid pilgrimage to her kinsman whilst on a visit to the Belgian Royal Family in the 1950s.

Notes :

1. Ypres Town Cemetery and Extension Cemetery holds British casualties mainly from October 1914 to April 1915. Others were added after the final actions around the town in April-May 1918. The military plot was enlarged after the Armistice by gathering together graves of those fallen in the area. A notable grave there is that of Lord Worsley, killed in action while manning his machine gun in a rearguard action at Zandvoorde on 31st October 1914. He was buried in a shell-hole by the Germans who dutifully recorded his burial, including an accurate sketch map locating his grave. The cavalry memorial at Zandvoorde marks the exact spot of this first grave. His remains were exhumed in 1922 and re-buried at the Ypres Town Cemetery and Extension. The graves lying alongside the wall on the Menin Road side of the cemetery include many of the headquarter staff of the British I Corps killed by shell-fire at their headquarters in Hooge Château in October 1914. Their horses were seen by a German plane, whose pilot reported to his artillery who immediately sent in a fatal barrage – the first time air observation had tangible effect in modern warfare.

2. The site of the action is easily identifiable as this part of Belgium has changed little since 1918. The road east from Zonnebeke continues across the Broodseinde crossroads toward Waterdamhoek and, after about half a mile, dips and then gently rises towards Keiburg atop the spur of high ground that bears its name. The action was broken off at the lowest point of the slope in the fields to the right of the road just after crossing the narrow Heulebeek which still trickles its solitary course today. The Keiburg was never disputed again by the British until late September of 1918 when it was captured in the final advance. It was from the Keiburg Spur that the German Staff ordered their troops into an abortive counter-attack to halt the Australians on the Broodseinde Ridge in October 1917. From here they also filtered in re-inforcements to overwhelm men of the 10th Battalion A.I.F. during the raid on Celtic Wood on the morning of 9th October 1917. *The Anatomy of a Raid* by Tony Spagnoly gives a full account of this tragic event..

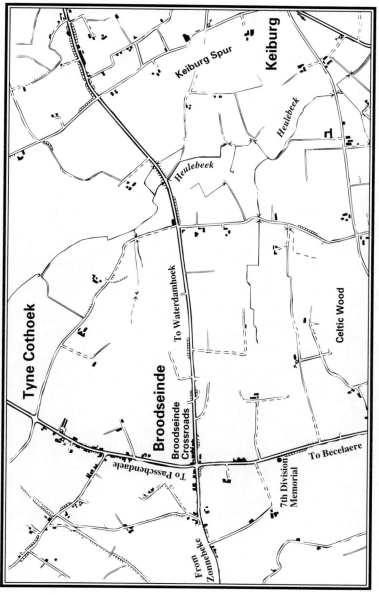

Prince Maurice was hit while leading his men across the crest of the ridge just south of the Broodseinde crossroads.

Petit Bois craters today are identifiable from the light tree growth around their edges. In the far distance to the right of the skyline can be seen Mont Kemmel.

6

MAJOR CROPPER'S CRATERS
Wytschaete, Messines ridge, 1917

IT IS COMMON CONSENSUS that one of the the most successful British offensives of the Great War was that which resulted in the capture in 1917 of the Messines Ridge, held by the Germans in a vice-like grip since the November of 1914. This escarpment of high ground had been one of their prime objectives in the early battles around the West Flanders town of Ypres in 1914. It stretched for a distance of approximately one mile between the villages of Wytschaete and Messines, and retention of this high ground allowed them clear observation and dominance on either side of it for miles, and particularly towards Mont Kemmel in the west, itself a key to the French northern industrial plain.

Planning by General Plumer's Second Army staff to secure this feature was of the highest calibre, much to the surprise of the enemy who were more used to the British lacklustre preparations of previous years. This time the art of mining would take on a new dimension. Begun in 1916 and completed to a disciplined timetable, the placing of twenty-five mines, culminating in nineteen of them detonating on 7th June 1917, took the enemy completely by surprise as his strong-points on the western slopes of the ridge were literally blown into the sky.

British, Irish and Anzac troops had expected bitter

contests on the heights after the eruptions but the advance went virtually unopposed. An encouraging feature of the operation was that casualties had been light, certainly when compared with past experiences and, for the first time in the war, Irish troops from the north and south, casting off old tribal loyalties, attacked shoulder-to-shoulder, and swept into Wytschaete village, clearing the adjacent woodlands of Petit Bois and Grand Bois at the same time. Wytschaete to the north had fallen to the Irish, the English 19th Division had cracked the vaunted position at Hollandscheschuur Farm and Anzac troops had penetrated and encircled Messines to the south, and all by seven o'clock in the morning. By early afternoon British, Irish and Anzac units had crossed the road along the crest-line and were digging-in on the reverse slope in preparation for expected counter-attacks. Troops all along the front had taken their objectives for the day. It has been a moment of unqualified success and not until the attack at Cambrai later on in the year would the allies feel the euphoria of such success again.

No figures are available to show the extent of the loss to the defenders after 957,000 pounds of explosives were triggered under their trenches at dawn on 7th June. At the close of the immediate fighting several thousand were unaccounted for, and that in addition to the casualty returns tendered by the various units. Over 6,000 were taken prisoner, many in such a dazed and shocked condition as to be unaware of their circumstances, so traumatic had been their experience on the Ridge.

Key participants in the implementation of the Messines campaign were a certain Major Cropper and his 250th Tunnelling Company. Today, a stroll or drive along a section of the old battle-line passes six craters blown by the Major and his company on the 7th June 1917.

Leaving the village of Wytschaete on the road to Kemmel, known as Suicide Road by the troops, passing a military cemetery and a Celtic cross memorial honouring the men of the 16th (Irish) Division to the right, and on past the mass of the Wytschaete Wood there, in a by-road to the right, sits Maedelstede Farm where one of the Major's craters lies close to the road's edge.[1] Its size, 205 feet in diameter, belies the fact that a charge of 94,000 pounds of ammonal made it the second largest mine exploded on the 7th June. The Maedelstede Farm position had always been seen as a tough nut to crack and the Germans retained a strong garrison at this sensitive spot. No serious attempt had been made to secure it since an attack prior to Christmas 1914 by the Royal Scots and Gordon Highlanders of the 3rd Division had been beaten off with serious loss to the attackers.

Continuing along this by-road and taking the next turning to the right, a short walk passes Vandamme Farm on the left with, due east and directly opposite, the twin craters of Petit Bois, now cattle watering pools in a woodland that in 1917 was a place of menacing substance. From a slope just behind Vandamme Farm sappers of Major Cropper's 250th Tunnelling Company dug to a depth of nearly one hundred feet to push forward their tunnels to Petit Bois, one of the strong outer-defences of the ridge itself. An attack here in late 1914 by the Royal Scots and the Honourable Artillery Company had proved a failure and no serious activity had taken place since.

Major Cropper worked his tunnels towards the opposing line with all the speed he could muster, but the texture of the Flemish clay proved to be a problem. Progress was painfully slow and the rigid timetable was in jeopardy as work proceeded through 1916 on into 1917. Then the staff responsible had an idea to help retrieve lost time. A boring-machine which had been used with good results during the construction of the London Underground was adapted by Thomas P. Headland Ltd., an engineering company in England. It was shipped to Flanders under conditions of great secrecy where it was hoped it could achieve some of the good results attained in England. Slowly and painfully the borer, weighing almost a ton, was assembled and put to work. At first the results were good and there was a mood of buoyant enthusiasm amongst the engineers as 200 metres of Flanders earth were quickly eaten up. However, problems soon arose as the villain of the piece, the Flemish mud, proved to be too doughty an opponent. Work slowed in the cloying conditions, fuses blew and the machine stalled. Temporary fuses were utilized using barbed wire, but these proved of little use and eventually it was considered ill-advised to carry on as valuable time was being lost in repairing the borer. It was abandoned to a muddy grave eighty feet beneath a Belgian meadow where it lies today, rusting away in solitude with its borehead pointing towards the old German lines.

Digging was recommenced along a new path and, by the spring of 1917, a 1,810 foot gallery with a branch-off of 210 feet had been extended under the strong-points along the western edge of the wood. Each chamber was tamped with charges of 30,000 pounds of explosives and the Petit Bois mines were ready to blow. Major Cropper had beaten the Flemish mud without the custom-built boring machine, but it had been a long and hard period, and not without tragedy. In the summer of 1916 he lost twelve men when the enemy, probing for the tunnels, blew a counter-mine channelled from a position in Petit Bois named Nancy Support. A large hole, probably a mine-working, can be seen today deep within the wood on the approximate location of Nancy Support. When the mines erupted on 7th June the Irish infantry of 49th Brigade fell upon the stunned defenders before the earth settled. The German front trenches, Nancy and Name, were soon taken as the Irish steamed through to join up with their victorious compatriots in Wytschaete just ahead.

Three more craters marked down to Major Cropper are at Hollandscheschuur Farm just ahead and right of where the by-road from Vandamme Farm meets the Vierstraat-Wytschaete road, the boundary between the 16th (Irish) and the 19th (Western) Divisions during the attack.[2]

A short walk along this road sees it take on a sunken nature where, just north of the German position Red Château[3], the Inniskilling Fusiliers sheltered from decimating enemy machine-gun fire laid down from Hollandscheschuur Farm to their left before regrouping and assaulting Unnamed Wood laying just ahead on the northern outer-protective zones of Wytschaete.[4] Hollandscheschuur Farm was captured by men of the 19th Division who fought their way over the Nag's Nose, a maze of fire-trenches and machine-gun posts on a lip of rising terrain in front of the farm, easily identifiable today with one of the craters commanding a central position on its crest. Three of Major Cropper's mines exploded here, eliminating the evil potential of the Nag's Nose for ever.

As well as those of the Major, visitors can still inspect other craters along the line embracing the ridge area, from

47

Hill 60 in the north to Ploegsteert Wood in the south. The one at Hill 60 is dry and shallow, not doing justice to its devastating eruption; its twin, the Caterpillar, is a peaceful lake enclosed by tall trees in private ground opposite; the mighty Spanbroekmolen crater was purchased for Britain after the Armistice and converted into a Pool of Peace and is much used as a reserve for anglers; and so on along the line – all nineteen are there, most brimful of water, and all peaceful and silent in startling contrast to their reason for being.

Notes :
1. In his book *Wet Flanders Plain* Henry Williamson describes how he and his wife in the early twenties argued with some Belgian youths in a café at Maedelstede Farm before being chased out, only escaping from the youths by jumping on a tram on its way from Kemmel to Wytschaete (The old tram system no longer exists).

2. The craters at Hollandscheschuur Farm are on private land and used for watering cattle. Looking westward from the farm toward the Kemmel-La Clytte road it is possible to pinpoint where the triple tunnel shafts were started behind a small group of trees edging the road running due north directly across the front of the old Nag's Nose.

Looking westwards from the farm towards to the hamlet of Vierstraat the ground lining the ridge is where the Army of the United States under British command saw action for the first time in the Salient in the summer of 1918.

3. Henry Williamson described prowling around the ruins of Red Château on Christmas Day 1914, finding a dead German sniper in an upstairs room.

4. It was during the attack on the woods at Wytschaete that Major William Redmond M.P. was fatally wounded. Unnamed Wood was renamed Inniskilling Wood honouring the men of the Irish Regiment who captured it on June 7th 1917.

48

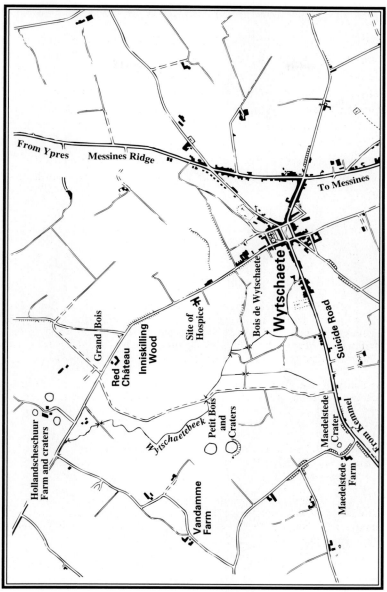

From Ypres

Messines Ridge

To Messines

Grand Bois

Inniskilling Wood

Red Château

Site of Hospice

Bois de Wytschaete

Wytschaete

Suicide Road

Hollandscheschuur Farm and craters

Wytschaetebeek

Petit Bois and Craters

Maedelstede Crater

Maedelstede Farm

From Kemmel

Vandamme Farm

Major Cropper's Craters are all visible today and within a comfortable walking distance of each other.

49

SGT. HARRY COMBES D.C.M, a postwar picture (1925).

50

The memorial to Keith Rae outside the walls of Sanctuary Wood cemetery. The inscription on the Memorial plinth (bottom picture) is misleading since the memorial was moved to Sanctuary Wood from its original site in the grounds of Hooge Château. (Cameo 2).

The Hooge Crater, the "ornamental pond", in the grounds which once embraced the old Hooge Château. (Cameo 2).

Looking across the R. E. Grave to Railway Wood from the old German front line in front of Bellewaarde Farm. (Cameo 3).

The grave of Major William Redmond M.P. with its distinctive headstone sitting outside the walls of the Locre Hospice Military Cemetery. (Cameo 4).

H. H. Prince Maurice of Battenberg's grave just by the side entrance to the Ypres Town Cemetery and Extension. (Cameo 5).

This is the happy warrior
...this is he
Herbert Read.

7

SERGEANT HARRY COMBES D. C. M., R.G.A.
Zouave Wood, Ypres, 4th October, 1917

A T DAWN ON THE 4th October 1917 prior to the opening of the offensive to capture the Broodseinde ridge, a key feature on the way to Passchendaele, allied troops waiting behind their tapes, and in the case of the Anzacs, in front of them, were surprised to be enveloped in a fierce German barrage. The fire was heavy and far-seeking and it was feared that the assembled troops had been observed and the enemy was indicating his intention to make a stand and halt the run of extraordinary successes enjoyed by the allies troops, especially the Australians, in the preceding weeks.

An enemy counter-attack at this juncture had not been anticipated and it was unnerving for the British observers to even contemplate that the offensive would be contested strongly by a rejuvenated enemy, supposedly on his knees after a string of recent reverses. All down the line enemy guns searched and probed, attempting to destroy the approach tracks which could be utilized by the British. Every copse and farm-building, every sunken road, fold and dip in the ground which could house troops, hide gun-batteries or afford shelter was battered unmercifully and received its fair ration of death and destruction sent over with the compliments of the House of Krupp.

The roads and tracks through the once wooded glades of Polygon and Glencorse Woods and the military road through Château Wood at Bellewaarde were turned into virtual death traps for the unwary as the barrage heralding the Germans' own counter-measure reached a crescendo. A large natural basin of ground in front of the Hooge Château and lake known as Dead Man's Bottom, a place known for the concentrating of infantry reserves, became a vortex of fire before the artillery ranges were lifted to play the last vestiges of hate through Railway Wood to end up on the Menin Road at Hell Fire Corner, almost at the gates of Ypres itself. It transpired from documents found after the Battle of the Broodseinde Ridge that the German intention was to mount a counter-attack to retake some of the ground lost to the Australians in and around the Polygon Wood area in the earlier September battles. The counter-attack was a dismal failure as the Australian infantry had laid-out in front of its tapes before zero hour and had started its move on the Broodseinde Ridge just as the German infantry began to move under its barrage to prepare for the attack. Although taking serious losses from the barrage, the Australians were first to recover their poise at this meeting on the lower western slopes of the ridge and put the Germans to flight after engaging them in a most brutal close-combat encounter. The interruption the artillery barrage caused to the British programme, although serious in its effect on increasing their casualty listing, a listing the allied troops could ill afford, had no effect on the overall result as the attack was a resounding success, resulting in the capture of the Broodseinde Ridge, making the 4th October 1917, to quote from German documents : "a very black day in all it's magnitude."

Many acts of gallantry and unrecorded bravery were enacted that morning along the line of fire, where

52

sweating, frightened men and animals flinched as they stoically endured the fearsome experience together. There is one act, fortunately well documented, which will allow an abiding memory of all those who died from the results of that fearful barrage at dawn on the 4th October 1917.

It occurred close to Hell Fire Corner at the extreme range of the German retribution. The fields around this infamous corner were being used for shelter by various groups of infantry and isolated gun batteries who must have thought themselves the target as the searching enemy fire grew closer. Several British artillery units were stationed in and around the slope leading up to the battered hamlet of Hooge and the large natural valley suitable for the siting of heavy guns that lay between Château Wood and Sanctuary Wood. From the sprawling mass of the latter stood a small section of woodland named Zouave Wood, so-called from more tranquil days when it safely sheltered French Colonial troops. It was now a smouldering, blackened mass of ruined trees and bushes housing a battery of heavy British guns and their sweating teams preparing to support the corps attack by Australian infantry on the Broodseinde Ridge several kilometres ahead to the east.[1] This unit, the 17th Heavy Battery, Royal Garrison Artillery, had just come up after a spell of duty on the Comines canal at the Spoilbank south of Ypres. The battery, with four sections of heavy guns, had a strength of over 200 horses and 160 men under the command of Major G. G. Walker and his second-in-command, Captain W. Fenn. They all held their breath in trepidation as the ranging enemy fire came nearer.

The Battery War Diary for dawn on the 4th October 1917 details clearly what happened next :

Our bombardment opened at 6 a.m. – but during the preparation for this at 5.50 a.m. enemy shelled battery position causing heavy casualties as follows:- Gunner Gimblet (killed); Gunner Calvert (wounded – but died during the day); Sgt. Combes, Gunners Tierney, Dunbar, White and Jolley all wounded and on to hospital. Battery and dug-outs heavily shelled during the afternoon.

A battery stalwart in this critical period, identified as wounded in the war diary, was Sergeant Harry Combes, a thirty-two year old regular from Chichester, Sussex. Harry was a battery sergeant of the old school, a professional soldier with years of service behind him, typical of the British non-commissioned officer of the time, the type of soldier who had made the army of the period a formidable force for the German Imperial Army to contend with.

Harry Combes now brought to bear his experience as, wounded as he was, he stood his ground, steadied the men under his command and, as the smoke cleared, saw them through those dangerous moments following such a tragic calamity. His darkly handsome features, apparent in photographs of the period, sternly epitomize the steadiness mustered at that moment of crisis in his battery's fortunes.

Although shaken and wounded himself, he ensured that the rest of the battery did not forget the job in hand, namely engaging the enemy gunners on the Broodseinde Ridge. When things had calmed down in the aftermath of the shelling Harry arranged for the removal of the dead and for the wounded to be taken for treatment. He then, and only then, sought aid for himself, probably at the Dressing Station close by at Birr Cross Roads on the Menin Road.

For his conduct and courageous example on this day Sergeant Harry Combes would be recommended for a well earned Distinguished Conduct Medal, the citation of which appeared in the *London Gazette* of January 1918 :

282298 Sgt. H. Combes, R.G.A. (Chichester).
For conspicuous gallantry and devotion to duty in keeping his gun in action under heavy fire of every description. One gun of his section was put out of action, and the remaining sub-sections were forced to withdraw to cover. He, however, stood fearlessly in the open in the rear of his gun and kept it in action against a hostile battery, thus setting a splendid example of pluck and determination to all ranks at a critical time.

Standing alone under heavy gunfire and keeping his gun in action! There were those awarded the supreme acclaim of the Victoria Cross for less.

After 6 a.m., when the British barrage had enveloped the German positions at Broodseinde and the Australians had begun to secure the ridge, the enemy counter-fire slackened and the smoke and flame cleared from the Menin Road and Hell Fire Corner area. The gunners began to clear up their shattered gun site and emerged into the fresher air to lick their lips, and to give thanks to whoever they considered responsible for their escape from the German barrage.

As for the hero of this little episode, Harry Combes, his thoughts would have been on many things as he moved rearward to receive some much needed medical attention. This well experienced, responsible and caring non-commissioned officer would view the morning's events with mixed emotions without knowing he was to be awarded for his gallantry. It had been a close-run thing but Sergeant Harry Combes would survive his wounds and the war to return safely to England and his family after the Armistice.[2]

He had endured the painful loss of two friends in action and several others badly injured. It was a morning that would live in his memory for the rest of his life!

Harry's two colleagues who died on that fateful day are buried in separate British military cemeteries in the Ypres Salient. Gunner Calvert lies in the Menin Road South Military Cemetery, Ypres and Gunner Gimblet in The Huts Cemetery, Dickebusch.[3]

The 17th Heavy Battery stayed in the Ypres Salient in a support gunnery role until the 28th October 1917, then transferred to First Army Reserve Corps near Bethune. Captain W. Fenn was in command at this time.

Notes :

1. The site of Zouave Wood can be located today, although it was never replanted after the war. It is now a meadow lying at the north-western edge of Sanctuary Wood, a few 100 yards due south of Hooge and the Menin Road.

2. Harry Combes returned to Chichester to be re-united with his wife and children but sadly passed away in 1930 at the age of 45. He is buried in the Chichester area.

3. The Registers of names for the Menin Road South Military Cemetery, Ypres and The Huts Cemetery, Dickebusch record :
Menin Road South Military Cemetery.
Calvert, Gnr. W. H., 84927. 17th Bty. Royal Garrison Artillery. 4th Oct., 1917. Plot II, Row J, Grave 10.
The Huts Cemetery.
Gimblet, Gnr. George, 65161, 17th Heavy Bty. Royal Garrison Artillery. Killed in action 4th Oct., 1917. Age 30. Son of George and Bessie Gimblet. Plot IX, Row C, Grave 10.

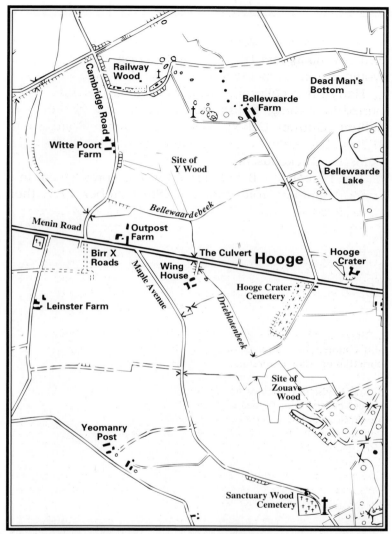

The site of Zouave Wood where the 17th Battery R.G.A was positioned on 4th October. 1917 and where Sgt. Harry Combes was wounded and awarded the D.C.M. The whole area shown on this map suffered under the German bombardment at dawn on the 4th October, 1917.

57

Photograph : Ted Smith

Rosenberg Château today. The Château was rebuilt on its its original footings on the lower slopes of Hill 63.

And I to my pledged word am true,
I shall not fail that rendezvous.
Alan Seeger.

8

A CEMETERY LOST
Rosenberg Château, Rossignol Hill, Ploegsteert Wood

THERE ARE OVER 450 burial grounds in Belgium honouring the allied fallen who gave their lives on the Western Front in the Great War of 1914–18. A total of 1,000,000 of the British Empire's finest manhood was lost on the battle-fronts, and approximately a quarter of those who fell did so around the historic town of Ypres. No society can sustain a loss on such a scale without suffering some adverse effect and perhaps even now, so far removed in time, those in Britain are still feeling the echoes of that vast bloodletting. New leaders who might have steered the nation throughout the unpredictable thirties were not there when needed, having perished during the merciless carnage of the Somme and Passchendaele. With a different leadership the Second World War may well have been avoided, and likewise the loss of another 250,000 young men, a reservoir of talent a war-torn and struggling nation could ill afford. This loss has never been captured more aptly than by the writer A. E. Housman when he wrote : "Here dead lie we because we did not choose to live and shame the land from which we sprung. Life, to be sure, is nothing much to lose; but young men think it is, and we were young."

The work of recording the vast legions of the dead in France and Belgium owes much to the leadership of one man, Major-General Sir Fabian Ware, who took measure of this task at the outbreak of war in 1914 when, in Belgium and France, he headed a miscellany of Red Cross 'flying units', later to be formalized as the Red Cross Mobile Unit. In 1915 he formed the Graves Registration Commission with part of its brief being to negotiate with governments of those countries where British dead had fallen to arrange for parcels of land to be ceded to them in perpetuity. In 1917 the Commission became the Imperial War Graves Commission and received the Royal Charter with the solemn and binding duty to care for the graves of men serving the Crown who had died on active service.

The British Government had already ordained that men of its forces killed on service abroad would be buried where they fell and, by virtue of an agreement signed at Le Havre on the 9th August 1917, the Belgium government had undertaken to acquire properties containing the burial plots from their respective owners in order that construction of permanent cemeteries could take place, leaving the sites immune for all time from local development.

During 1917 Sir Fabian Ware consulted various authorities in the areas of design and architecture to establish the form to be given to these British military cemeteries sited in foreign fields. The consensus was that they would portray an equality in death both for officers and other ranks and they would contain a uniform headstone, memorial tablet and cross, all similar in design, construction and dimension. The headstone was to display the cap badge and a religious symbol, the latter of which which would be determined, or omitted, at the request of the family. The Cross of Sacrifice designed by Reginald

Blomfield and the Stone of Remembrance, designed by Sir Edwin Luytens with its inscription *Their name liveth for evermore,* selected by Rudyard Kipling, would all constitute components of the basic styling of the cemeteries. They would be uniform, dignified and respectful, establishing havens of peace and meditation for the pilgrims who would come in future years to view the fields of battle, or to pay respect to those who gave their all.

The impression to be created was that of a garden, with herbaceous borders, flowers and plants from England of a growth that local conditions would allow. The concept met with public support and, after three cemeteries of this style created in France were favourably evaluated, the scheme was adopted universally.

The British system of burying their men where they died resulted in a schematic of cemeteries of various sizes springing up along the old front line, resembling a tragic necklace of white stone. Size was no impediment or barrier, and they ranged from the largest of 11,956 graves at Tyne Cot in Belgium, down to one of the smallest of nearly forty graves comprising a group of young Canadians who fell around the Beehive pill-box on the Plain of Douai near Willerval on the Arras battlefront in France. Smaller groups of British graves can be found in many communal plots sited in villages where, thanks to the good offices of the local population, and in grateful thanks to the allies for the sacrifices made by their young soldiers, the British were allowed to use plots adjoining civilian areas.

The Le Havre Treaty of 1917 defined that the 450 war cemeteries in Belgium would be inviolate. Inscriptions were to be featured in each cemetery, engraved in English, French and Flemish proclaiming the land in question had been ceded in perpetuity, thus relatives need harbour no fear that graves would be disturbed. Their loved ones would remain at peace for all time. This principle would apply in all the countries where the Commission's remit prevailed. The Commission adhered firmly to its principles and charter until, in June 1930, they were called upon to implement, until then, an unheard-of task. They were being obliged to close a cemetery plot and its extension, exhume the fallen therein, and remove the bodies to another cemetery. The owner of the land on which the plots were sited had contested with the authorities in leaving the British fallen within the confines of his estate.

The plots were Rosenberg Château Cemetery and Extension located in private estate grounds close to the village of Ploegsteert. Rosenberg Château, the name an anglicised version of Villa Roozenberg, was situated within the grounds of the baronial estate of the Hennessy family nestling on the slopes of the looming Hill 63[1] close to the Messines Ridge within sight of the leafy mass of Ploegsteert Wood, also part of the estate.

The cemetery was started there in November 1914 by units of the United Kingdom when sporadic fighting and skirmishing had taken place in the area before the trench-lines were permanently formed. It lay close to the main house which had been shelled and destroyed by fire on the 14th of the same month. In May 1916 an extension was started and used mainly by Australian and New Zealand units who found a much-needed use for it in the spring of 1917 during the build-up to the Messines offensive. Within range of enemy guns for most of the war, the villa, or château, was used for first-aid stations, dug-outs and various headquarters catering for neighbouring units loitering within its confines. The two cemetery plots were called Red Lodge, identifying with the name given by the troops to the dressing station set up within the château and its surrounds.

The owner of the château returned to his property after the Armistice with intent to rebuild the shattered house as his family residence. It was his contention that the military plot so close to his home would detract from the amenities of the property and would hardly create the best ambience within which to raise his family.

His point of contention worked its way through various official channels and became a cause of some concern and discussion at meetings held regularly in Brussels with members of the Anglo-Belgium Committee. The matter was left unresolved for some time before developing into an emotive issue between the two former allies. The Belgian Minister of the Interior was forced to intervene when questions on the subject were raised in the respective parliaments, and letters of concern, some quite heated, appeared in the national press of both nations. However, the Minister, whose position corresponded with that of the British Home Secretary, whilst holding a wide range of powers of persuasion, had none which he could call upon to coerce the owner of Rosenberg Château who, under Belgian law, was acting strictly within his rights.

The owner absolutely refused to be persuaded to permit the bodies of the fallen Australian, British, Canadian and New Zealanders to find a permanent burial place on his land, and he remained stubbornly obdurate under pressure from many local and national sources. To have fought the matter through the Belgian courts would have meant certain and humiliating legal defeat for the British

Government, so, much to the sorrow of the commission, and particularly so to its vice-chairman, Major-General Sir Fabian Ware, there was no other course but to acquiesce and arrange for the removal of the bodies.

During the lengthy period of legal wrangling the graves at Rosenberg Château had been dutifully maintained by the Commission's gardening staff, but work of a permanent construction nature had not gone ahead as the Commission in its wisdom had foreseen the possibility of defeat in the matter and had anticipated the consequent need to remove the bodies and close the cemetery.[2]

The High Commissions and governments of the dominions from whose countries the fallen had originated were made fully aware of the painful decision, and it was with their sad approval together with that of the British authorities that the remains of their sons and those from the mother country were removed and re-interred.

On a sombre autumnal morning of 1930 each soldier was exhumed and, under military honour guard with flag-draped transport, took his short but final journey down the château drive to the bottom of Hill 63 where, accompanied by the plaintiff notes of the Last Post, he was laid to rest in the Berks Cemetery Extension at the Hyde Park Corner crossroads on the edge of Ploegsteert Wood.[3]

Thus were buried 475 men from the United Kingdom, Canada, Australia and New Zealand, casualties mainly from the years 1914 and 1915.

They found their final resting place in a cemetery already containing the graves of 394 men. It was here in 1931 that the imposing Ploegsteert Memorial to the Missing was erected, featuring the names of 11,447 men who fell but who have no known graves.[4] These were men who had met their fate at Armentières, Aubers Ridge, Estaires, Fromelles, Hazebrouck, Outtersteene and on the Scherpenberg, the high ground near Locre.

This spot reflects so well the quality of care and consideration conducted by staff of the Commonwealth War Graves Commission. The cemetery and monument appear to be in the same pristine condition they enjoyed when first erected over half a century ago. The commission's work continues winter and summer, year after year, with no effort spared to make this a worthy resting place for those who lie here, and especially so for those whose places of rest were disturbed and moved here from Rosenberg Château[5]

Notes :

1. Hill 63. The crest of this tactically important hill can be reached from a pathway starting on the road running west from the Hyde Park Corner crossroads. From the summit, a clear view of the Douve Valley and the Messines Ridge is afforded and many traces of artillery positions and dug-outs are evident. The hill is honeycombed with shelters and tunnels. The Australians excavated a complex system called The Catacombs here – it is still within the hill but its entrances have been lost and entry is not possible.

2. During the period when the situation on the Rosenberg Château plots was being resolved, Sidney C. Hurst, P.A.S.I. was deeply involved in the production of his admirable work, *Silent Cities*. This excellent book was published in 1929 and Rosenberg Château cemetery is identified on its reference map (map 14, page 36) as number 1917. The section at the rear of the book, Index to Cemeteries, page 359, does not feature the reference number or any detail relating, an unavoidable omission made necessary at the time of publication and, sadly, never to be rectified.

3. The register of the Berks Cemetery Extension Rosenberg Château plots, number B 339, was published in 1925, before the bodies were moved, with the map at the beginning of the register showing the original position of the Rosenberg Château Cemetery and Extension.
4. On the opposite side of the road to the Rosenberg Château reburials

is the Berkshire Regiment cemetery wherein lies Lieutenant Ronald Poulton Palmer of the 1/4th Berkhires. He was killed at Anton Farm north of Ploegsteert Wood on the night of the 4th/5th May 1915. Palmer, a member of the biscuit family from Reading, Berkshire, was an international rugby player of some repute, captaining England several times and playing his last game for England against the French in Paris in 1914. In the same row of graves is Private Giles of the 1st/4th Berkhires. He was the first fatality recorded by the Berkshires having died of wounds when caught by shellfire whilst undergoing trench maintenance instruction on the edge of Ploegsteert Wood in early 1915. He was buried a few days before Poulton Palmer. Also in that row of graves is a 16-year-old rifleman of the King's Royal Rifle Corps. Private A. E. French was hit by shellfire in 1916 while undergoing instruction. His story was the subject of a BBC radio programme entitled *He should not of been there should he?*. based on the letters of his sister of Wolverton, Buckinghamshire The Hyde Park Corner (Royal Berks) Cemetery register of graves records :

French, Rfn. A.E., C/7529. 18th Bn. K.R.R.C.,15th April, 1916. B.2.

Giles, Pte. Frederick William, 3053. 1st/4th Bn. Royal Berkshire Regt. Died of wounds 28th April, 1915. Age 17. Son of Frederick James and Sarah Giles, of 9, Hilcot Road., Reading. B. 13.

Poulton Palmer, Lt. Ronald William. 1st/4th Bn. Royal Berkshire Regt. Killed in action 5th May, 1915. Age 25. Son of Professor Edward Bagnall Poulton and Mrs. Emily Palmer Poulton, of Wykeham House, Oxford. B. 11.

5. The Rosenberg Château was rebuilt on its original footings and can be seen from the first by-road to the right off the the road running west from the Hyde Park Corner crossroads, just past Underhill Farm Cemetery on the right. The by-road winds its way up the hill, offering an unimpeded view of the rebuilt Château. The main residence of the baronial estate within which the Rosenberg Château cemetery was located was called La Hutte Château and today, rebuilt on a site just close to its original, maintains it's air of affluence. Ruins of the original buildings are identified in dramatic profile on the rising ground on the right as the road from Messines sweeps round to Hyde Park Corner cross-roads. The cellars of the original Château were used by various allied units and apparently still exist. It was owned by the Hennessy Cognac family, as was Ploegsteert Wood, then part of the estate.

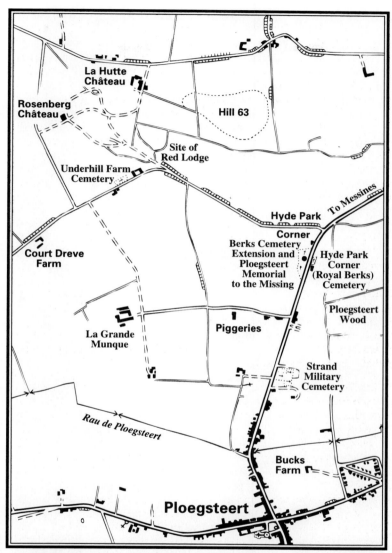

Rosenberg Château and its surrounds were used as a dressing station, named by troops as Red Lodge as were the Rosenberg Château Cemetery and Extension.

CAPTAIN RONALD RIOCH DAVIDSON.

Out here the dogs of war run loose,
Their whipper-in is Death;
Across the spoilt and battered fields
We hear their sobbing breath...
M. A. Bell.

9

A SCOTTISH SOLDIER
Captain Ronald Rioch Davidson 2nd Battalion, Royal Scots,
St. Eloi, Ypres, 1916

O N THE EVENING OF the 28th March 1916 a middle-aged pharmacist practising in Montrose, Scotland, died of a heart attack. His grieving widow, with four of her children still at school and nobody to run the family business, sent an urgent cable to the War Office enquiring whether her eldest son, a serving officer with the Royal Scots on the Western Front could be granted compassionate leave. To her surprise a telegram arrived the following day stating in stark terms, "The War Office regrets ...".

Captain Ronald Rioch Davidson had just passed his twentieth birthday when he was killed by a solitary German shell crashing down out of the evening air on 27th March 1916 as he led his company into the line at Shelley Farm, St Eloi, exactly twenty-four hours before the death of his father, one of the many tragedies that afflicted thousands of British families during the violent course of the Great War.

It is ironic that one shell falling from the heavens during an otherwise calm and inactive period can seek out and destroy a valuable young life. This unfortunately was an all too familiar scenario played out during the war years.

The level of bloodletting during that war was quite incomprehensible to those looking back from today's perspective. Nearly twenty per cent of Britain's menfolk were involved in service of some sort, and 750,000 of them were to die, a factor of nearly one in five, a statistic that poses the question as to what society might have been without that massive loss. Life was cheap on the Western Front, and it was said that a subaltern subjected to the rigours of trench life had an even chance of surviving six to eight weeks. Captain Ronald R. Davidson, 2nd Battalion Royal Scots, would do better than average. He would survive the bloodiest of fighting in the Ypres Salient from June 1915 until his death in March 1916, a period of nine months.

Born in Montrose on Christmas Eve, 1895, the eldest son of Alexander Davidson, a pharmaceutical chemist, his circumstances were comfortable if not affluent within a happy family environment headed by his mother Jessie. He had two brothers and a sister, Harold, Gordon and Bessie. Harold, aged twenty, was fated not to survive the war. Wounded at Bullecourt Station Redoubt near Bapaume in August 1918 while serving with the 2nd Battalion London Scottish, he was rushed to a base hospital but died en route.[1]

Academically Ronald proved to be very bright, attending Montrose Academy, a prestigious local place of learning. He was described as "extremely clever, quite ambitious and fiercely competitive" by a contemporary and plans for his future were taking shape. In 1913, at the age of seventeen, he was awarded the James Duke Medal for being a distinguished scholar and, in early 1914 when barely eighteen, he was honoured by being named the best student at Montrose Academy, sealing his success when awarded the Dux Medal, a much sought-after badge of acclaim. In the following months, whilst reading arts at

70

the University of St Andrews, insight prevailed upon him to join the University Officer Training Corps in case he were to be called upon in view of the worsening European political situation. When the Balkans flashpoint exploded into war Davidson suspended his university studies almost immediately and enlisted.

After a short period of training, taking into account his academic accomplishments and O.T.C. experience, he was offered a commission in the 12th (S) Battalion, Royal Scots, an early Kitchener unit under training in the Edinburgh area. His commission was confirmed on the 27th November 1914 just as the first battles of Ypres reached their bloody but vital conclusion. His training with the battalion in that first winter of the war filled him out in body and spirit. In May 1915 he was deemed ready for active service and was sent to a replacement depôt where officers were fed to line battalions.

This was the period in 1915 following the end of Second Ypres where the Germans had used poison gas for the first time, applying tremendous pressure on the British line defending the town. Casualties among battalion officers and non-commissioned officers had been serious and it was against this backdrop of events that, on the 23rd June, Second Lieutenant Davidson crossed to France.

After a few days at Le Havre base camp he was moved up the line, one of many to make up the severe losses recently incurred. He joined the 2nd Battalion Royal Scots, part of the 8th Brigade, 3rd Division at a camp in the Brandhoek area north of the Poperinghe-Ypres road. The battalion, commanded by Lieutenant-Colonel J. Duncan, a career officer, was having a much-needed rest after a particularly traumatic period manning the trench-lines around Hooge Château for a period of twenty-five days. During this time there had been fierce fighting in which the 2nd Battalion incurred 150 casualties. Second Lieutenant Davidson joined at an opportune time since he was able to familiarize himself with the unit and get to know his fellow officers as well as the men who would be under his command.

Serving in C Company under a much respected Captain R. S. Stewart, he settled in as a platoon officer and had his baptism of fire at Hooge in late July. The hand-to-hand fighting flowed back and forth in and around the Château and stables as frenzied enemy counter-attacks were repulsed after the blowing of a large mine under the strongest part of their position. It was here the enemy introduced liquid fire, taking ground warfare into a new form of frightfulness.

Adding to his battle experience, Second Lieutenant Davidson served short terms at St Eloi and The Bluff, both near the Ypres-Comines canal and, from contemporary accounts, acquitted himself well.[2]

On 25th September the battalion was destined to take part in an operation which would prove to be one of trial and suffering. The scene of the action was the northern fringe of Sanctuary Wood facing the Menin Road, the 25th being chosen to coincide with the opening day of the Loos offensive further south. The action was a diversionary tactic intended to apply pressure on the enemy, thus preventing him transferring men and guns which were sorely needed on the Loos battle front. It would be a day of intense activity all along the British line and, for the 2nd Battalion, an ordeal and a long, tempestuous but successful day. C Company were engaged at various contested points in the right-hand sector of the line. Almost cut off at one stage, the battalion fought its way through three lines of enemy trenches along the infamous Menin Road, taking 116 prisoners of the XV Prussian Corps in the process. However, early advantages were nullified as gaps appeared on the British flanks and the enemy, with skilful use of bombers and élite reserves, retrieved much of the lost ground. Casualties had been heavy in the 8th Brigade but the Royal Scots could congratulate themselves on having played a gallant part in the proceedings.

The fighting continued for a day or so before it petered out on the Hooge front – but the Germans were not satisfied with the situation and on the 30th September penetrated the British line inside Sanctuary Wood to the right of Hooge. The 2nd Battalion was sent over to Maple Copse to help shore-up the line and, with the 4th Battalion Middlesex and 2nd Battalion Suffolks, attacked, but to no avail against such a resolute foe. The fight was called off with the 2nd Battalion taking another 100 casualties. One of those killed was their much respected and popular C Company commander, Captain Stewart. This redoubtable officer was described on the day as "the bravest of the brave".[3] His loss was a blow to the battalion and particularly so to young Davidson who, under his example and guidance, had been able to assimilate easily into life at the front. When the actions concluded, the battalion, in need of rest and recuperation, having taken over 250 casualties, was moved to a new camp at Reninghelst south-west of Ypres, there to lick its wounds and await re-inforcements who would need a period of intense training in order to meet the standards of efficiency required by the Royal Scots. The camp, provisionally named I Camp, lay alongside the Reninghelst-Westoutre road and was described in the battalion war diary as a "veritable sea of mud". Davidson was among a group of eighty-five officers and men employed for the sole purpose of making this forlorn site fit for habitation during the long bleak winter months ahead which would be used for refitting and refurbishing the battalion.

That winter was relatively quiet. No major battles disturbed them, only the business of taking its turn in defending the vulnerable and sensitive trench system around the crossroads at St. Eloi, south of Ypres on the Wytschaete road. These crossroads were dominated by an ominous mound, a tactically important twenty-five foot high spoil heap, the remains of a local brickworks. It provided invaluable observation for the Germans over all the British positions from Bois Quarant in the west to the canal sector in the east and had been in German hands since the early days of the war. Machine-gun fire from it made life difficult if not highly dangerous for anyone raising his head above the parapet.

Life during the sullen wet months of a Flemish winter was soulless and dispiriting. So much so that a return to the limited shelter and warmth of their Reninghelst camp seemed like a brief trip to heaven. The village provided the chance to eat a better fare and the estaminets must have been crowded with brave young men grabbing a brief experience of civilization away from the ever-present dangers in the line. On the 6th December Davidson would have been pleasantly surprised and honoured to be informed of his promotion to acting captain, a sign that his general conduct and bearing since joining the battalion six months before had been recognized.

1916, the last year of Ronald Davidson's short life, dawned quietly with the battalion fulfilling its duties at St. Eloi. The battalion headquarters was in the nearby village of Voormezeele and periods out of the line were spent in their camp at Reninghelst. The men had a rare treat in the first week of March 1916 when they were given a moment of brief respite in the comfortable houses of Poperinghe. Captain Davidson and men of C Company were housed in the Burghers' villas in the Rue Carnot and here they would have enjoyed the more tranquil and safer existence experienced in the rear areas. This would be a blissful interlude from the steady drain of casualties which life in the trenches of St. Eloi represented. This was followed by a short tour of duty at the Bluff craters where again the battalion took casualties – casualties which it could ill afford in view of an operation being planned for the 3rd Division.

On the 27th March divisional staff ordered an attack at St Eloi where they intended to explode six large mines under the German positions. Men of the 8th Brigade were to secure the enemy trenches, including the Mound under which the largest charge was to be laid. The mines were blown on time and, on the right flank of the attack, the lst Battalion Northumberland Fusiliers left their trenches before the mine debris had fallen and were far too quick for the dazed defenders. The Fusiliers fell upon them with verve and enthusiasm and soon had craters numbered 1, 2 and 3 secure in British hands. The Mound was no more. It had been flattened and its eighteen-month grip on the sector was a thing of the past. However, serious problems had developed on the left flank of the brigade front. Owing to a permutation of poor light, heavy mist, accurate machine-gun fire and a swiftly applied counter-barrage, the 4th Battalion Royal Fusiliers had floundered badly. They lost direction in the murky visibility and, in the face of ferocious fire, had veered away from their objectives, crater numbers 4 and 5, thus leaving an exposed gap which the enemy was quick to spot and even quicker to exploit. The Royal Fusiliers had been stopped in their tracks, taking heavy losses. They could only make the best of a bad job and, picking up as many of their wounded as they could, limped back under withering fire to their trenches near Shelley Farm and from there called for urgent assistance.

During this mayhem the 2nd Battalion Royal Scots had been in brigade reserve in Scottish Wood near Dickebusche about two miles distant.[4] Reinforcements were received, one of them being a young officer, Second Lieutenant McTurk-Rainie, nineteen years old and the son of a Scottish aristocrat who Captain Davidson now welcomed to his company. Second Lieutenant Rainie had arrived from Scotland barely twenty-four hours before. The battalion, with its new second lieutenant, was ordered to the front line and rushed to the village of Voormezeele at 7 p.m. on 27th March. In gathering darkness C and D Companies set off across the fields towards Shelley Farm to relieve the weary Fusiliers. Time was of the essence in case the enemy, suspecting any weakness after the morning's fighting, should take advantage and push ahead and, as the road from Vormezeele to St. Eloi was exposed to German shell-fire for much of the way, it was felt more prudent for C Company to enter the Convent Lane communication trench that led-off left across the fields.[5]

For Second Lieutenant Rainie this would be his first time in action. He, together with his "veteran" companion

Captain Davidson, led their men towards the firing line just ahead, silent now except for the sizzle of a flare here and there and the isolated crackle of a rifle shot as a nervous sentry peered into the gloom. There had been sporadic shelling earlier in the afternoon, but the main actions of the day were at an end and neither side seemed in the mood for more. The men began to breathe more easily as they approached the ruined farm, preparing themselves to relieve the Royal Fusiliers anxiously waiting to get out.

What happened next is a mystery, an act of God perhaps. Somewhere in the German lines near Wytschaete or beyond the canal at Hollebeke, a nervous German gunner loosed off a shell into the night sky. Down it came with all its blazing venom, straight into the path of the incoming C Company.. When the smoke cleared Captain Davidson, Second Lieutenant McTurk-Rainie and three other ranks lay dead. For Davidson, fate had caught up with him after nine months. For the tragic Rainie, his war was over before it had begun.

Twenty-four hours later the Royal Scots were relieved by the 2nd Battalion Suffolk Regiment, having had a quiet day and incurring no more casualties. It made its way back sadly to its Reninghelst camp on the 28th March taking along five dead comrades – true sons of Scotland with so much to offer, so much to fulfil.

The two young officers aged nineteen and twenty years had barely known each other a full day. They had shared a short but unique brotherhood in circumstances of extreme adversity, their destinies bound in a common act of sacrifice,

Captain Ronald Rioch Davidson and Second Lieutenant James Wilson McTurk-Rainie lie next to each other at

Reninghelst New Military Cemetery in Plot I, Row D, Grave 12 and plot I, Row C, Grave 12 respectively.

A Soldier quiet and silent now.
Only he can tell me why
The woods are green in April
and young men born to die.
Do you feel the spring I wonder
neath the turf that you lie under
Though the thunder and the sunshine
only reach you as a sigh.

Notes :
1. Harold Davidson lies at the British Military Cemetery of St. Sever, in Rouen, Normandy, France.

2. Such was his standing in the battalion that in September 1915 Ronald R. Davidson, still a Second Lieutenant, was selected to parade a battalion honour guard near Dickebusche when brigade units were inspected by General Sir Herbert Plumer, G.O.C. Second Army, and Lord Kitchener, the British Minister for War.

3. Captain Norman Sinclair Stewart was killed on the 30th September 1915. As many men as could be spared from the 2nd Battalion Royal Scots attended his burial in the British Military Cemetery at Vlamertinghe. He lies in Plot I, Row G, Grave 2.

4. Scottish Wood is still in place just east of Dickebusche Lake. It was named by men of the 10th King's Liverpool (Liverpool Scottish) when they were at rest there.

5. The Convent Lane communication trench, due east of the outskirts of the Voormezeele, ran north of where the Bus House British Military Cemetery is located today.

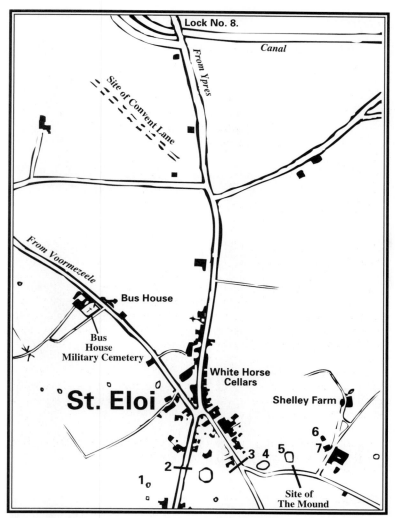

Of the infamous craters at St. Eloi, numbers 1, 4 and 5 can still be seen today. 2, 3, 6 and 7, no longer identifiable, were sited approximately in the positions shown above. The Royal Fusiliers, who C Company were about to relieve when Capt. Davidson and 2nd Lt. McTurk-Rainie were killed, were sheltering in trenches near Shelley Farm just north of Craters 6 and 7.

Photograph : Ted Smith

Pick House today sitting amongst a row of houses on the right hand side of the road to Messines just outside the village of Wytschaete.

I am awake. I am alive. There is a bell sounding
with the dreams retreating surf.
Herbert Read.

10

ALONG THE MESSINES RIDGE
The Ypres Salient, 1914 – 1918

THE ROAD FOLLOWING the crest of the Messines ridge runs due south from the village of Wytschaete to that of Messines. On the right of the road between two of the houses skirting Wytschaete sits a German shelter, square, neat and very clean. Although covered by ivy and other foliage it is recognizable as a German structure with its opening facing east towards what were his rear areas in 1917. The British lines at that time stretched along the lower western slopes in what was the front of the shelter but which now constitute fields belonging to local farms and back gardens of the houses lining the ridge. This fine example of a German defence-line building is all that remains of the Pick House strong-point, a large menacing complex of enemy trenches and small forts which spanned this section of the ridge, evidence of the Germans' determination to keep a firm hold on the Messines Ridge.

This small reminder of the strong-point was probably a command bunker, ideally sited on the crest road to receive despatch riders or infantry runners and it is not difficult to imagine the bustle of activity that would surround such a place during the war years.

These defences part-covered the higher western slopes of the Messines Ridge, giving the ever watchful enemy observers impressive views and an excellent field of fire over the British positions to the west, right back to the strategically important village of Kemmel.

At dawn on the 7th June 1917, the British offensive opened with the blowing of nineteen carefully sited mines. Immediately following the explosions the demoralized enemy was in no condition to offer anything but minor resistance in this sector as, stunned and battered, he fell back before the rampaging advance of the English, Irish and Anzac infantry. It was the 36th (Ulster) Division who attacked up the slope towards Pick House, and its verve and enthusiasm was too much for the defenders to contend with as they struggled to come to terms with the mighty eruptions which had shattered their nerves and broken their line. By 8.30 a.m. the Irishmen had crossed the crest road and established posts on the reverse slope fully 2,500 yards from their start-off point near the old mill at Spanbroekmolen where one of the largest mines had been fired.[1] The Pick House system had been one of the main objectives of the Ulstermen, whilst their southern Irish counterparts winkled-out the defenders in the woodlands in and around the nearby village of Wytschaete. The defenders, quality, battle-hardened troops, resisted gallantly for a time as the dust and smoke from the explosions began to fade and clear. They had a good field of fire but they had reckoned without the dash of the Irishmen. The 10th Battalion Royal Irish Rifles, moving swiftly with grenade and bayonet, fell upon the outer line of rifle pits and machine-gun posts and subdued large sections of the Pick House complex with minimal casualties to themselves. Many prisoners were taken including a battalion commander and his staff who surrendered, perhaps at the very bunker we can see today.

The brief flurry of action subsided and the complex of trenches and forts was left isolated as a backwater when the British line advanced and reformed in the valley on the eastern reverse slope of the ridge. The Germans were expected to react but the counter-attacks never developed with the anticipated intensity and the British were left to consolidate and strengthen their new line in comparative peace for the next nine months. The Pick House flirtation with notoriety was not over. It flared into prominence again when, in April 1918, it lay in the path of the enemy as he developed his push towards Kemmel. His determined advance across the River Lys south of Armentières smashed through the Portuguese corps holding the line at this point. His intent was to reach the industrial plains of northern France and he was prepared and ready to steam-roller all opposition to achieve this aim.

In the second week of April 1918, German corps under the command of General Von Arnim launched heavy ground attacks along the Messines Ridge and the sprawling mass of Ploegsteert Wood in a bid to reach Kemmel and its commanding height, Mont Kemmel. The weather was misty, a sound advantage to the attackers, while the British along the ridge, and particularly around the village of Wytschaete, were being hard-put to keep abreast of the fast-changing situation as the enemy offensive developed. This drive towards Kemmel and Armentières had to be delayed. Should the British forces be split, there would be nothing to prevent the enemy reaching the town of Hazebrouck and then on to the coast, leaving no doubt as to the fate of the allied armies in Flanders and France. Enemy patrols and skirmishers moved in on Pick House to gauge possible resistance and found the 10th Battalion Royal Warwickshires of 19th Division in residence and, perceiving a strong chances of a breakthrough here, intensified the pressure.

Many of the Warwickshires were young draftees, hardly trained, and certainly untried in battle. The divisional history refers to them as "merely boys" who had been rushed out from Great Britain. Nevertheless they were stout-hearted and, with their ranks stiffened by experienced veterans, gave strong account of themselves, but the enemy made good progress and was exploiting gaps appearing in the line with a great deal of success.

The 9th (Scottish) Division ordered its South African Brigade, heroes of Delville Wood two years before, to counter-attack to relieve the hard-pressed Warwickshires. On the 10th April the South Africans, taking advantage of mist and poor visibility, mounted their attack. Disregarding heavy enemy fire the 2nd Battalion South African Regiment (Natal), and the 4th Battalion South African Regiment (South African Scottish) moved on Pick House and Messines respectively. The fighting was fierce and bloody, with the 2nd Battalion, under the command of Captain Jacobs, attacking at a point the enemy was determined to hold. Pick House now took on the stance of prime tactical importance.

The South Africans' efforts were fierce and determined, but the overwhelming numbers of enemy reserves denied them the ultimate prize of taking the line. They had delayed the Germans' advance in this sector until the 12th April and by then the British had established their new line of defence between the heights of Messines and Kemmel.

The South Africans incurred casualties of 639 of all

ranks within the space of thirty-six to forty-eight hours. Shades of Delville Wood repeated, but their sacrifice had bought the British the valuable time needed to avoid the splitting of their forces.

The military significance of Pick House was now finished for all time. It was never fought over again in the conflict.

The Germans, with nothing to impede them, mopped-up the remainder of the ridge and headed for Mont Kemmel to the west. Here, in a brilliant attack by their Alpine Corps, they surprised the French defenders of the hill and captured it. The industrial areas of northern France were now opened to them and they went on to capture the towns of Bailleul and Armentières. Now the railhead town of Hazebrouck and the coastal ports beckoned to them, and General Haig saw fit to proclaim his famous "Backs to the wall" message.

The situation facing the British was now critical but, in the final count, it was saved by the unparalleled bravery and gallantry of the British Guards, 33rd and 29th Divisions and the classic defence of Hazebrouck by the 1st Australian Division, rushed up from the Somme front to play its part in the dramatic events of that time – but that is another story.

On the eastern side of the Wytschaete-Messines road, along a minor road branching off almost opposite the ivy-covered Pick House, lies the entrance to Torreken Farm cemetery.[2] Sited in a field lying behind a private house, this small military cemetery houses men who were casualties of the Messines offensive in June of 1917. The first were buried here that summer, probably dying of wounds at the medical post which existed here. The farm gave its name to the general area shown on trench maps of the time and was used by the British in late 1917 and early 1918 as a place of rest and recuperation. The regimental history of the 13th (S) Battalion Rifle Brigade, 37th Division, responsible for the locality in the late summer of 1917, notes : "The men enjoyed a period of long rest at Torreken Farm Shelters.".

To the rear of the cemetery is a slightly raised area of broken pastureland marking the site of a large underground shelter with its entrances blocked-in and its ventilation outlets visible above ground level. Enemy dug-outs abounded in this area east of the Messines Ridge and this is almost certainly one of them. A local farmer was able to relate that, before the Second World War, visiting German veterans who served here as stretcher-bearers had said the site had been one of their advanced dressing stations. Its position in the safe lee of the exposed ridge makes this a credible proposition and it can be assumed that, when the enemy were forced to withdraw after the successful attack on the Messines Ridge, the British in their turn made full use of the vacated facilities, the cemetery being a legacy of this. This is a truly evocative site to visit and it is hoped that modern developments will leave it sacrosanct as this underground shelter will remain one of the finer relics of the Great War artefacts to be found on the old Western Front.

Within half a mile or so of Pick House and Torreken Farm is another military location worthy of note. A small woodland known as Onraete Wood with a farm complex at its rear lies on the left-hand side of the road running north-east of Wytschaete towards to the village of St. Eloi. British map-makers of the time chose to retain its Flemish name rather than designate one of common military usage.

On the 24th April 1918 this wood saw one of the most heroic episodes of the critical Battle of the Lys, during which the Germans tried desperately to break the British line, split the allied command and force a retreat towards the Channel ports. This particular day saw British units battling to halt the vastly superior enemy forces in their attempt to take the Messines Ridge area and advance towards Kemmel and northern France. General Haig's "Backs to the wall" message to his forces on the 21st April had stiffened resolve, and this would now be demonstrated by battle-weary men of the lst Battalion East Yorkshire Regiment, 21st Division, manning the shallow fire-pits and trenches around the edge of Onraete Wood. The Battalion, having been in action for several days, were tired, grimy and weary beyond belief. A professional unit with several years experience of war in Europe, it was now being subjected to one of the heaviest bombardments it had experienced. For over three hours its area was saturated with shellfire of all calibres as the Germans approaching the Messines Ridge area sought to destroy all opposition before them. All approaches to the Onraete sector received a battering as the barrage cut off all sources of supply and reinforcement. The area was drenched in high explosives and gas as communication links were broken, telephones destroyed, and movement of any sort was restricted to scurrying from one place of shelter to another. The Yorkshiremen steadfastly held the line as, to all intents and purposes, the little wood was cut off from assistance of any kind, leaving them isolated. Under covering fire and smoke screens, the advancing Germans edged into the wood from the direction of

Wytschaete and Torreken Farm expecting an easy passage with little or no resistance. They were to be disappointed. The thin line of East Yorks rose from their positions and stood their ground, raking the now not so jubilant Germans with accurate rifle and machine-gun fire. The enemy was taking heavy casualties as time and time again he reformed to rush the edge of the wood only to incur more casualties and be driven back once more by the determined East Yorks. Nevertheless, the pressure was beginning to take its toll on the thin line of defenders and at one particular stage it weakened and almost broke when, as recorded in the regimental records, a lone, unnamed N.C.O climbed on to the top of one of the pill-boxes sited in and around the perimeter of the wood and, alone and unprotected, held the Germans on his immediate front by working his machine gun unsupported. It was an heroic act of the highest order, and it saved the situation, the unknown N.C.O. no doubt being awarded the grateful thanks of his beleaguered comrades but not those of his country. With valuable time gained and the Germans temporarily halted, the surviving Yorkshiremen began an orderly retirement across the nearby Wytschaetebeck stream in the general direction of Mont Kemmel and their spirited resistance came to an end. Battalion losses had been tragic with only three officers and thirty other ranks finding their way to their lines and safety. The Brigade diarist recorded : "They all fought at their posts... and died there."

That stark, simple military assessment of the heroism displayed by the East Yorks at Onraete Wood is the only tribute and monument to honour the men who fought and died there. The fallen were buried by the enemy as they cleared the area, probably in one mass location soon after the dust of battle cleared. It is hoped the Germans afforded full honour to those fallen Englishmen.

Onraete Wood was replanted after the hostilities and the farm rebuilt on its original location at the rear. The pill-box witnessing the brave act of the lone, unnamed N.C.O. was demolished in recent years when the site next to the wood was developed into a garden centre but several German shelters and pill-boxes remain in the wood, grim memorials of the day the Yorkshiremen made their stand against a marauding horde.

The ambience of this emotive spot may be spoilt for many by the bustle of the busy garden centre now doing its business next door, but this should not mar a visit to an historic and interesting, if mainly forgotten, piece of wooded ground. It is a place of pilgrimage in the fullest sense. Stand within the confines of this quiet wood and let your thoughts range to those desperate days, and to the men who sacrificed all on that one dramatic day in the April of 1918. Remember them. Most are there still.

Notes :

1. Now known as the Pool of Peace the Spanbroekmolen crater was purchased for Britain in the 1920s and is used extensively by local anglers. On the western side in a nearby farmyard is Lone Tree Cemetery. Begun in June 1917 after the explosions, it holds 88 graves, 60 of which are of men of the 36th (Ulster) Division. Many were killed by falling debris in No Man's Land as the mines erupted. Lyn MacDonald describes well this incident in her book *They Called It Passchendaele*.

2. Torreken Farm Cemetery was begun in June 1917 when the area was secured after the Messines offensive. It was started by men of the 5th Dorsetshire Regiment and was used by British units until the April of 1918. It contains 90 British and Australian graves from that period. One interesting casualty here is 17 year old Second Lieutenant Paul John Rodocanachi, 53 Squadron R. F. C. who made his first flight in the first week of July 1917 and only two weeks later on the 27th was shot down

over Wytschaete with his observer Second Lieutenant N. L. Watt. Both young men are buried next to each other here. Although right of entry to the Torreken Farm military cemetery plot is official, as with all British military cemeteries under the care of the Commonwealth War Graves Commission, it is located within private farming property and care should be taken when crossing the field in the middle of which it is to be found. Apart from the farmer being occasionally a little unfriendly, menacing and generally uncooperative, it has been known for bulls to graze in this particular field and, because they seem to follow the farmer's general disposition, they caused one of the authors of this book to leave his camera tripod behind when making a more than hasty exit after one particular visit. It is assumed that the tripod is now hanging on the farmer's wall as a Great War trophy. The house alongside the path leading to the field (not the farmhouse itself which is located on the northern edge of the cemetery) at one time housed (and may still) a number of dogs who, like the bulls, did not seem to recognzse the right of entry mentioned earlier and, although not certain, it can be assumed that those animals have never heard of the Commonwealth War Graves Commission.

Just along the track from Torreken Farm cemetery is the larger Derry House Cemetery. It contains approximately 126 graves of soldiers from the United Kingdom and 37 from Australia (29 of whom belonged to the 47th Battalion). Derry House was the name of the farm which stood here and was captured in June 1917 during the Messines action. An interesting feature just outside the walls of the cemetery is a finely constructed German pill-box or shelter where a long forgotten member of the workforce who built it has left his glorious mark on history by leaving a perfect imprint of his hob-nailed boot in the pill-box cement covering. What better comment by someone engaged in such a labour of love. This shelter extends into a barn within the farm complex just outside the cemetery walls and this part is in almost perfect condition. It has retained its pristine appearance due to being covered and left in peace all these years. The barn is put to regular use by the farmer and it is necessary to seek his permission to visit this superb example of German military architecture.

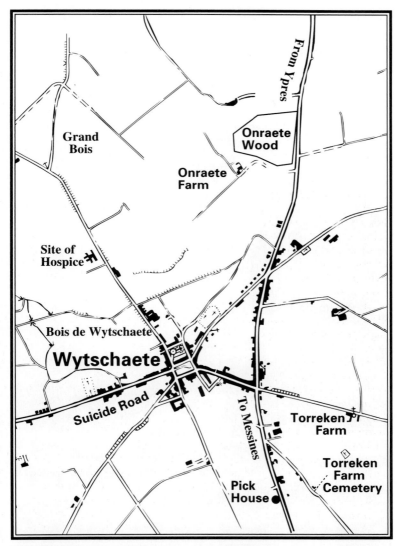

Grand
Bois

Onraete
Wood

Onraete
Farm

From Ypres

Site of
Hospice

Bois de Wytschaete

Wytschaete

Suicide Road

To Messines

Torreken
Farm

Torreken
Farm
Cemetery

Pick
House

This quiet section of the road running from Ypres, past the village of
Wytschaete (White Sheet to British troops during the 1914-18 period)
and on to Messines holds many concrete memories of the Great War.

The London Scottish memorial on the right-hand side of road from Messine to Wyrtschaete.

His wild heart beats with painful sobs
his strain'd hands clutch an ice cold rifle.
His aching jaws grip a hot parched tongue
Herbert Read.

11

HALLOWE'EN NIGHT 1914
The London Scottish at Messines

A S THE FIRST BATTLE OF YPRES entered its final stage, the
hard-pressed British Expeditionary Force blunted the
German drive on the historic town of Ypres. Repeated
attacks from Langemarck in the north to the Messines
Ridge in the south had been thwarted by the heavily
outnumbered, thin line of khaki. Had it broken, the
Kaiser's Imperial Army would have split the Anglo-French
command in Flanders and driven on to the Channel ports
virtually unopposed. With mounting losses, and at great
sacrifice, Sir John French's small, professional force refused
to concede ground, and that "Contemptible Little Army"
entered the annals of military history by thwarting the
political ambition of one Kaiser Wilhelm II.

The tide of combat had ebbed by the end of November
1914 to leave what was to be known as the Ypres Salient,
embracing the town of Ypres and its environs from
Dixmude near the Belgian coast to Ploegsteert Wood near
the Franco-Belgian border. Many actions had been fought
to reach the conclusion to First Ypres. The King's Royal
Rifle Corps at Keiburg, the Guards at Klein Zillebeke,[1] the
Black Watch south of Langemarck, the dismounted cavalry
at Hollebeke, all played their part in stemming the tide. It
had been a struggle, but the line held. It had sagged and
stretched in places, but nevertheless held.

The 31st October 1914 saw men of the 1st London Scottish, commanded by Lieutenant-Colonel G.A. Malcolm, become one of the first British territorial units to see combat, helping impede the enemy advance along the Messines Ridge and barring his way westwards to Kemmel and northern France. Other territorial units had seen action, notably the Honourable Artillery Company at Wytschaete – a minor affair compared to that enacted on the night of the 31st October along the heights of the Messines Ridge. The London Scottish sold their lives dearly when they battled to prevent this part of Belgium from being eaten up by the Teutonic juggernaut.

As light faded and the moon cast a pale glow over the ridge area on this historic Hallowe'en, German troops, singing and shouting, massed on the eastern foot of the ridge and rushed the slopes with bugles blowing and bands playing to add impetus to their advance. They expected little opposition from the thin screen of battered defenders. How wrong they were and what a lesson they were about to learn. "The hour maketh the Man", a dictum of much truth when applied to those Scots under their baptism of fire, carving for themselves a glorious slice of military history that Hallowe'en night in 1914.

On the 28th October they had been at St Omer in northern France, then the British Army Headquarters garrison town, when they received orders to move up to the line. At 5 p.m. on the afternoon of the 29th they boarded a convoy of thirty-four London buses and drove to Ypres arriving at 3 a.m. on Saturday the 30th. At 6 a.m., after a brief rest in the Cloth Hall, they paraded and marched up the Menin Road toward Hooge, eventually mustering in Sanctuary Wood. They were to assist in the fighting at Gheluvelt but new orders informed them they were not needed as enemy attacks the had been thwarted. They spent the afternoon at Hooge before returning at 5.p.m. to the Cloth Hall in Ypres only to find the buses waiting to take them to act as reserve to the 2nd Division Cavalry holding the high ground linking the eastern edge of the ridge in front of Ypres to the Wytschaete-Messines ridge south-east of St. Eloi.[1] Again they paraded, this time at midnight, ready to moveup the line but these orders were cancelled as it was agreed that they needed rest after their continuous movements over the past days. At dawn on the 31st they at last moved into the line on the south-eastern slopes near St. Eloi and started to dig their fire trenches. At 8 a.m. orders arrived demanding their presence in assisting the 4th Cavalry Brigade on the Wytschaete-Messines ridge, so off they marched down the St. Eloi-Wytschaete road halting just south of the hospice in Wytschaete itself. They moved from here towards Wulvergem then turned left into the hollow of the Steenbeck and into a small valley named Val d'Enfer on the eastern slope of the ridge. Here they sheltered in a small woodland, L'Enfer Wood, set up their headquarters and awaited further orders.[2] At about 10 a.m. they moved in three lines, under heavy howitzer and shrapnel shell-fire, up to the crest where, adding to their casualties, they were met by rifle fire. Their orders were to support the 6th Dragoon Guards (Carabiniers) on the right of centre of the line and fill a gap in a position marked by two farms on the western side of the road, Huns Farm and Middle Farm.[3] A windmill was sited just north of the latter on the eastern side of the road.[4] They dug front and support fire trenches straddling the ridge-top road and, under constant bombardment, waited. When, at 9 p.m., cheering and shouting, the enemy attacked, their historic date with destiny was about to unfold.

The London Scottish, mostly recruited in the London area, had a high pre-war establishment and was trained to a high standard.[5] Nevertheless, to the men warfare was possibly a "barney" on a Saturday night, more serious when Scotland played rugby against England at Twickenham. The type of warfare in which they were now engaged was new, but they rose to their task magnificently.

As the unsuspecting enemy reached the high ground the London Scottish rose from their shallow trenches and drove them back, inflicting heavy casualties. More losses would have been incurred had the rifles of the Scots not proved to be defective. A recently adapted magazine spring would not move the bullet into the breech so the Scots, in combat for the first time, were using their rifles as single-loaders. Under bombardment until midnight they awaited the renewal of the attack they knew must surely come. By now the farms, the windmill, the hedgerows and haystacks in the surrounding fields were ablaze and, in this cauldron of fire, they were to experience a Hallowe'en they would never forget. In this blazing light and in bright moonlight, the enemy attacked in dense waves. Again cheering and with their bands playing "Deutschland, Deutschland über Alles". Again they were held, this time for about an hour as the Scots beat off rush after rush of the overwhelming mass of grey-clad infantry. The attack finally exhausted itself and there was a brief lull until about 2 a.m. when infantry of the 2lst RIR and 122nd Fusiliers Regiments piled on the pressure, rushed in once again and drove home their attack. Fierce hand-to-hand combat saw both sides contesting the crest road with the struggle becoming hectic and confused as the irregular line swayed back and forth. The fighting was hard, bayonets were crossed and rifle fire was at close quarters. Gradually the line was driven in, the Scots being forced inch-by-inch down the slope to the rise above Val d'Enfer where the attack was held.

The pressure was too much and, to save the territorials from complete destruction, they were ordered to withdraw towards Wulverghem. They had fought magnificently, given the enemy a severe knock, temporarily halted his advance and forced him to reorganize and regroup. The Germans in their hour of triumph chose not to interfere with the retirement. They had suffered enough and set about consolidating their newly won position, not prepared to tangle with the London Scottish any more. To quote the Scots' regimental historian : "They (the London Scottish) had borne themselves well." Thus the remnants of the 1st Battalion left the blazing ridge glowing in the night sky and gathered at the crossroads of Kruistraat before deploying for rest and refitting at the village of Dickebusche.[6]

What had they earned by their spirited defence at Messines? The Germans had been halted at a vital period in their advance and had been forced to reorganize and rethink their plan. After this severe shock, they were happy to hold what they had. Thoughts of further advances toward Kemmel and northern France were dispelled. The Messines Ridge was theirs, and would remain so for the next two and half years. But at what cost to the London Scottish? When Lieutenant-Colonel Malcolm reviewed his depleted battalion at Kemmel, 394 men of all ranks were casualties, killed, wounded or missing, but the Regiment had emblazoned on its colours "Messines, 1914" as a battle honour and the name would for ever be associated with those men of the 1st Battalion.

The final word goes to Sir John French forwarding the following commendation to Lieutenant-Colonel Malcolm in early November 1914 : "You have given a glorious lead and example to all Territorial troops in France.".

From *The Ypres Times* Vol. 2. No. 4. October 1924.

Unveiling of the London Scottish War Memorial
Messines, Ypres May 1923

A detachment of officers, pipers and a hundred men of the London Scottish had come out for the unveiling of the Cross to commemorate their comrades who fell in the charge at Messines on October 31st – November lst 1914; to commemorate also those who died in many subsequent engagements in France and Flanders, Salonica and Palestine. Messines is a tiny village perched towards the right-hand extremity (looking eastwards) of the salient, about six miles from Ypres, and about two miles nearer the end of the lip than Zandvoorde. The famous Hill 60 is near it, Kemmel Hill forming the extreme limit of the ridge. Here, as Lord Haig vividly explained at the subsequent ceremony, this regiment of civilians, each of whom proved later to be of the mould and grit of a hard-bitten veteran, were sent into action, almost straight from London, at one of the most critical moments of the first battle of Ypres. The Germans got their range, and shelled them with a cold accuracy, enfilading them besides, and taking deadly toll of the Scots. The regiment, covered with glory, found itself at once ranked with the most seasoned and reliable troops in the British Army. It was the memory of this great deed that the monumental Cross was erected to perpetuate.

The King of the Belgians had promised to do the Regiment

the unique honour of coming to unveil it himself. The rumour had gone round the night before that His Majesty intended to make the journey from Brussels, a hundred miles away, by aeroplane. Everything on wheels had been requisitioned to take us out from Ypres to Messines; and on a brilliantly clear morning we stood expectant on the top of the ridge, peering into the blue reaches of the horizon. Quickly, two specks appeared in the azure, which proved to be the Royal aeroplanes. They made long circuits high above us, then landed some distance from the scene. As the King and his staff approached along the cobbled road, Earl Haig (Honorary Colonel of the Regiment), Colonel Clowes (its Colonel), five former commanding officers during the War, and the Honorary and Acting Chaplains, went out to meet him. It was, indeed, a romantic dropping of Majesty from the blue – a unique experience, which none of who saw it is likely to forget. The King had performed the long flight in the space of one hour, and he was back in Brussels, we were told, ere the morning ended.

After presentations and the inspection of the troops, a religious service was begun, the Rev. D. C. Lusk, M.C., the gallant Acting Chaplain of the Regiment, conducting it. Then the King pulled the cord, and revealed the beautiful monolith, with the St. Andrew's Cross sculptured on top of it; and laid at the foot of the monument a giant wreath, bearing his own name and Queen Elizabeth's. Immediately thereafter I who had known in the old days so many of the fallen, said the prayer of Dedication and later gave the Blessing. King Albert made a long and most kindly speech from the steps of the pedestal, spoken in slow but perfect English. His kingly height and presence reminded me of the imposing figure of his noted uncle, the late King, whom I had seen on one or two occasions many years ago. The King's speech, and that of Lord Haig, who followed him, dwelt in detail on the long story of British valour with which the ridge would be for ever associated. Then followed the touching ceremony of placing wreaths at the foot of the Memorial by relatives of the fallen; the Lament was played by the pipers, and the Last Post and Reveille were sounded. Again a Belgian Regimental Band played the National Anthems. Ere the King left, he had all the men bought to him who had taken part in the battle, and spoke to and shook hands with each of them. It was all over in little more than half an hour. But it was a great day for the London Scottish, whom the Belgian King had chosen, out of all other British regiments, especially to honour. Many a ruin still testifies to the dire destruction wrought by the ruthless invaders. But in the long last, Belgium is still free, its industries, its people happy, grateful and prosperous. At a price our gallant brothers bought them this freedom; but the price had not been grudged.[7]

Notes :

1. Front-line transport was not allocated to the London Scottish. In their move up the Menin Road they were offered that of the 1st Battalion Coldstream Guards who had been virtually eliminated as a battalion in earlier fighting defending Ypres. At St. Eloi, they had no second-line transport and their quartermaster commandeered three of the London buses to carry rations and supplies. Could one of these busus have given its name to Bus House and the present-day cemetery of the same name sited just off the cross-roads at St. Eloi?

2. L'Enfer (Hell) Wood, on the slopes of the ridge to the east of where the Spanbroekmolen crater is today, was not replanted after the war.

3. Huns Farm (Four Huns Farm) has been rebuilt on its original site.

4. The Windmill, burnt to the ground, was never rebuilt and the the London Scottish memorial now stands on its original site.

5. Among the London Scottish ranks was Ronald Colman a former clerk in the city of London. His war lasted barely one hour. He was hit in a leg early in the fight and hauled himself off for treatment. After the war he found fame in Hollywood, but carried the scars of Hallowe'en 1914 for the rest of his life.

6. The Kruistraat crossroads where the London Scots gathered is where three of the mines opening the Battle of Messines exploded in 1917.

7. When the King of the Belgians landed below the Messines Ridge in 1923 to unveil the memorial it was one of the first recorded occasions that a reigning monarch used air transport to fulfil an official function.

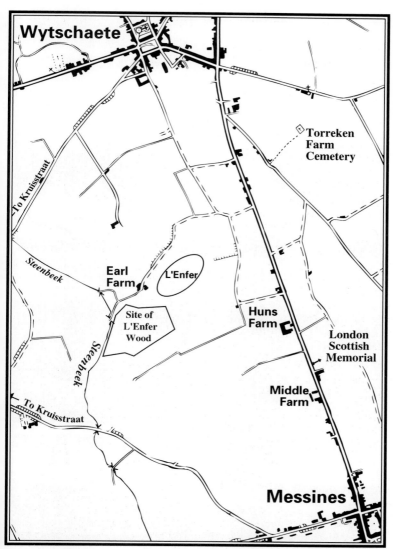

The Memorial to the London Scottish on the road to Wytschaete from Messines is sited on the spot of the windmill that, as with the surrounding farms, was destroyed by fire on Hallowe'en Night, October 31st 1914.

Photograph : Ted Smith

Prowse Point Military Cemetery showing its commanding view over Mud Corner Cemetery from where this photograph was taken.

Violets from Plug Street Wood
Think what they have meant to me
Life and hope and love and you!
Ronald Leighton to Vera Britain 1915

12

A BLOODLESS VICTORY
Prowse Point, Ploegsteert Wood, Ypres, 30th October 1914

PROWSE POINT BRITISH MILITARY CEMETERY stands on a prominent rise overlooking the northern edge of Ploegsteert Wood, a sprawling mass of woodland approximately nine miles south of Ypres.[1] The site of the cemetery was named after Major C. B. Prowse of the 1st Battalion Somerset Light Infantry who instigated an action here on the 30th October 1914.[2]

Major Charles Bertram Prowse, a career officer, had arrived with his regiment in France soon after the outbreak of hostilities in August 1914. The regiment had seen action in the battles at Mons and Le Cateau and was active in the retreat south under the scorching summer sun to the River Marne, and almost to the gates of Paris itself. It had played its part all through this gruelling campaign and was among the first units to recross the River Aisne and dig in on the north bank in time to halt the advancing enemy.

Major Prowse, then commanding B Company, caught the attention of his superiors in the 11th Infantry Brigade in this action and was cited in a special mention for applying "Initiative and brave good leadership". During the middle of October 1914 at the end of the period historians have categorised the "Race for the sea", both combatants had moved masses of men and material in a bid to gain tactical advantage, and the first trench-lines were dug, culminating in a fortified stalemate stretching from Nieuport on the Belgian coast to the Franco-Swiss frontier.

In October 1914 the Somersets, still part of the 11th Infantry Brigade, were based in and around the general area of Ploegsteert Wood with their battalion headquarters in an estaminet at Hyde Park Corner crossroads near the north-western corner of the wood. Some of their trenches crossed the spur of ground on which Prowse Point cemetery stands today, and from here they had excellent observation over the enemy lines below them in the wide, shallow valley of the River Douve. To their north lay the distinctive church tower at Messines on the crown of the famous ridge and, to their south, they commanded a view of Ploegsteert which screened the large industrial town of Armentières in northern France beyond.

The enemy had stepped up his efforts to crack the British defences around Ypres, the key to West Flanders, and the first battles around the town from the Menin Road in the north to Ploegsteert Wood itself in the south were reaching a critical stage. His activities became almost frantic as he perceived his momentum to be slowing down in face of the stiffening British resistance all along the line.

On the 30th October all appeared calm in the Somersets' sector even though gun-fire could be heard to their north from where the British were attempting to hold the ground between Wytschaete and Messines. To some observers the calm was almost unreal and a battalion narrative records : "The men certainly feared that this was the calm before the storm".

It certainly was! At 7 a.m. the Germans attempted to penetrate the defences around Ploegsteert as the Somersets made their way to the shelter of Hill 63 after being relieved by the Hampshire Regiment, their brigade partners. The relief was only half complete when the enemy put down a bombardment, launched an attack in force and began to penetrate the line along the road where today's cemetery is sited.

A breakthrough would have serious consequences for British positions further south and the Hampshires, not fully settled-in after relieving the Somersets, were taking casualties. The implications were obvious and those at headquarters realized that instant support was needed if the line was to be held and a precarious situation reversed.

The bombardment continued well into the afternoon and the British defence was barely taking the strain. Major Prowse, acting as battalion commander at headquarters, sent up his A Company to assist the Hampshires who by this time were suffering very heavy losses in their partly destroyed line. A Company arrived just as the enemy were crowding into the Hampshire trench line and, in fading light at around 4.45 p.m, a certain Second Lieutenant V. A. Braithwaite organized the erection of a barricade to impede the enemy rush and with a small group of men "gave a gallant defence of the position, until further help could be sent. "[3]

A battalion observer noted : "We had expected that we should a good gruelling next day (Oct 31th) and we did. The beauties of dawn had never appealed to me; on this particular occasion they were particularly unattractive. Dead Saxons were laying close to the front of the trenches, and some were actually in the road behind our support dug-outs. This particular section was considered the worst in the line. It was situated on a lip of high ground, the possession of which would dominate the village of St Yves and Ploegsteert Wood and was, consequently, a particular objective of the enemy's heavy artillery, variety known as 'Jack Johnsons' and 'Coalboxes'".

At 5.30 p.m. as darkness fell Major Prowse made a critical decision. Following messages received from battalion runners indicating that resistance by his A Company and the remnants of the Hampshires battalion was weakening and a breakthrough by the enemy was imminent, he personally reconnoitred the position and decided to mount a counter-attack that night with two of his companies, leaving a third as battalion reserve near headquarters. He led the attack himself, opting for no supporting barrage and with his men carrying only small arms and bayonets. The tactic was a complete success. The enemy were overcome by the speed and ferocity of the attack which cleared the roadside trenches and farm buildings close by. The marauding enemy quickly vacated the area, retiring to its defence line in the valley below.

The Somersets incurred no casualties! The attack, set up and effected with a finely balanced mixture of desperation and dash, had succeeded without the loss of one man. The break in the Ploegsteert Wood line was a thing of the past.

The action resulted in a "Bloodless Victory", for the Somersets that is, and Major Prowse was awarded the D.S.O. and promoted to Lieutenant-Colonel.[4]

Sir John French, noted the event in his despatches thus :

On the evening of 30th October, the line of the 11h Brigade (Brigadier-General Hunter-Weston) was broken near St Yves (St Yvon). A counter-attack carried out by Major Prowse with the S.L.I. restored the situation. For his services on this occasion this officer was recommended for a special award.[5]

To stand alone at the Prowse Point Military Cemetery

today reflecting on the events of the 30th and 31st October is a sobering experience. The British trenches under dispute at the time lay alongside the road in front of the cemetery, the spot where Second Lieutenant Braithwaite erected his barricade. The view from this tactically important lip of high ground sweeps over the River Douve valley to the north and beyond to the ridge-top village of Messines with its distinctive church tower silhouetted on the horizon. To the south the view takes in the gentle slope down to the brooding mass of Ploegsteert Wood which itself cloaks the approaches to Armentières in northern France. It was up this very slope, then a fire-swept slope, that the Somersets surged forward to ease the pressure on their beleaguered colleagues and to beat off a determined enemy. Who can tell what would have happened if the Germans had consolidated this position? If they had, then another determined thrust would have seen them at the gates of the industrial plains of northern France.

Major Prowse ensured this did not happen. His bold initiative cannot be evaluated in terms of changes of events that could have resulted had his attack failed. But it didn't fail, so all is left to conjecture. The fact that he succeeded, and without the loss of one man, defies all description within the context of the Great War and it is doubtful that an attack of such importance ever succeeded at such minimal cost throughout the remainder of the conflict.

Notes :

1. Prowse Point British Military Cemetery was used from November 1914 to April 1918 and holds 215 graves of men from the United Kingdom, Australia and New Zealand, 1 from Canada and those of 12 German prisoners. Another cemetery, Mud Corner Cemetery, is sited down a nearby track at the edge of the wood which led to its northern

entrance and was much used for the movement of men and supplies. Created by the New Zealand Division after their capture of Messines in 1917 it contains 85 graves of men from Australia and New Zealand and 1 from the United Kingdom. It is also the official entrance to the British plots within the wood.

2. A German soldier who would influence world events in future years was also in action in the Ypres Salient on the day Major Prowse led the attack at Ploegsteert. He was a corporal in action at Gheluvelt in the First Battle of Ypres, serving with the German 16th Reserve Infantry Regiment (Bavarian). Later in the November 1914 he won an Iron Cross while tending his wounded officer at Wytschaete just north of Prowse Point in an action at Bois Quarante. His name was Adolf Hitler.

3. 2nd Lieut. A. V. Braithwaite, 1st Batt. S. L. I., the son of a serving divisional commander, was killed in action at the Quadrilateral Redoubt on the Somme. His name is on the Thiepval British Memorial to the Missing. His family erected a memorial on the site of his death where it stands today beside the Serre Road British Military Cemetery (Somme).

4. Lieut.-Col Prowse D.S.O. went on to greater things. As well as Prowse Point being named after him, a farm on the Frezenberg Ridge near Potijze was named Prowse Farm to commemorate his activities there during 1915. He was promoted to Brigadier-General in 1916 taking command of his old formation, the 11th Brigade (4th Infantry) Division. At the opening of the Somme offensive he was wounded near the Quadrilateral on the Serre Road whilst attempting to move the attack forward and died the next day. He was first buried near Vanchelles, a small village on the Somme, before being moved to the British Military Cemetery, Louvencourt (Somme) where he rests today.

5. St Yves, the hamlet to the east of Prowse Point, is the birthplace of 'Old Bill', created by Bruce Bairnsfather whilst serving as a Machine Gun Officer with the 1st Royal Warwick Regiment. Two water-filled mine craters to be seen alongside the road between St. Yves and Hill 63 resulted from two of the smaller mine eruptions set off at the outset of the Battle of Messines in 1917. These were the mines laid from Trench 122, the southerly mines laid to support the attack on the ridge.

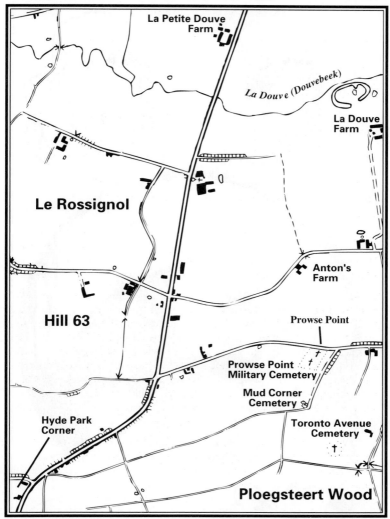

Prowse Point Military Cemetery marks the site of Prowse Point. Its position on the St.Yves-Hill 63 road commanding a view over Ploegsteert Wood to the south and the Douve valley to the north gave it a particular strategic importance desired by both the British and the Germans.

110

13

OLD BILL IS BORN
St. Yves, Ploegsteert Wood, Ypres, January 1915

I T IS SAID THAT HUMOUR is a weapon in the fighting man's armoury that, like everything else, doesn't "come up with the rations". If this be true, and it is a major ingredient in the upkeep of the front-line soldier's morale, then the British infantrymen lying out in wet trenches around Ypres had it in abundance in the winter of 1914.

It would be soon after the Christmas truce that a podgy, unshaven visage, bedecked with walrus moustache and tousled hair crowned by a battered military cap, began to appear on the walls of cottages, barns, dug-outs and an assortment of scrap paper. Depicting one man's conception of the professional Tommy Atkins, this stoic found favour with both officers and troops alike. His popularity spread like wildfire along the British line. His laconic, down-to-earth and matter-of-fact approach to life in the front line appealed to them. In their predicament they needed an outlet, and in Old Bill they found the ideal vehicle.

His homely if potently caustic utterances on a spread of subjects, prompted many a smile amongst weary men trying to maintain morale in the depressing uncertainty of trench life. Here one moment, entering the portals of eternity the next, laughter and lightheartedness did not come easy. When Old Walrus Face, as he came to be known, had an opinion on mud, rum rations, rats, shell-

111

fire, snipers, 'orrible Fritz over the wire, or his own "orficers", then out came the outrageous comments, prompting many a smile from the hardies, grasping hot mugs of tea in the icy dawn of a Flemish winter.

Old Bill was born in the winter of 1914 in a ruined cottage at Ploegsteert Wood and was destined to pass into immortality as the ultimate weapon of the British soldier. Even if German Intelligence had been able to discern the subtle change taking place among its enemy, the Teutonic character, not noted for its humourous content, would have been unable to counteract this phenomenon.

Old Bill was the brainchild of Second Lieutenant Bruce Bairnsfather a machine-gun officer with the 1st Battalion Royal Warwickshire Regiment, part of the 4th British Infantry Division.[1] It was responsible for the sector around the north-east corner of Ploegsteert Wood when, blinking grumpily and flaring his nostrils in the damp Flemish air, 'Old Walrus Chops' first saw the light of day.

His creator was born in Simla, India, in 1887 of a military father, then a professional soldier in the Cheshire Regiment. Bruce showed an artistic talent at an early stage amusing fellow pupils at the various schools he attended with his drawings. On leaving college he found it difficult to settle and, after stints as a commercial artist and a sales representative, his wanderlust took him to Canada where he hoped fame and fortune awaited him. Then in the August of 1914 war broke out in Europe.

In the general flurry of excitement and national euphoria he returned to England to enlist and join his fellow countrymen in what they innocently perceived to be the Great Adventure. By virtue of earlier experience gained with the Cheshire Militia, he became a prospect for immediate commission. It was this cycle of events which culminated in his prowling around the perimeters of Ploegsteert Wood on wet nights, squelching through thick mud to check on the men for whom he was responsible.

These were the early days of warfare which had just entrenched into the soggy stalemate it was to adopt for the next four years and Bairnsfather was experiencing it in the Warwickshires' sector between Ploegsteert Wood and the nearby slopes of the Messines Ridge. He had enjoyed the unique experience of the Christmas truce of 1914 when carol-singing, exchanging gifts and playing a rudimentary game of football with the enemy, brought the British and their Saxon cousins together in No Man's Land to pray, bury their dead, and generally celebrate the birth of the Prince of Peace.[2] This truce must have seemed ironical to many among that gathering. A brief moment of goodwill, and then back to the trench-lines to get on with the war.

Bairnsfather might have contemplated such events as he trudged in his solitude on the many dark and stormy nights following the wet and tortuous route around his allotted gun positions. These were spread over a tract of battlefield from the corner of the wood to the towering mass of Hill 63 and the well-known junction of trenches called Hyde Park Corner about a mile to the west.[3] It was not a pleasant experience after a day in the trenches to have to do these nightly rounds. Slipping and sliding in the cloying mud, usually cold and wet from the incessant Flemish downpours, he would have been taunted by the vision of horizontal figures swathed in blankets, snoring away in blissful slumber in the many dug-outs he would have passed. Behind the protective curtain cloaking the warm inner glow, he would have envisaged the eternal tea bubbling on the Tommy cooker. A warming "cuppa" would have lit his dampened spirits, albeit briefly, before he needed to wrap up, venture out into the winter elements and complete his round of nocturnal duties.

He found these tours depressing and nerve-wracking. It was during one of them that he had the germ of an idea that was to change the course of humour in the war and dramatically affect his life and circumstances. His route back to the muddy hole, the dug-out he shared with his soldier servant, took him past the group of ruined cottages which comprised the little hamlet of St Yves lying along a small perimeter track on the extreme edge of the wood, sporting a small pond where it met the road to Hill 63.

He knew that the ruins housed fellow officers of his brigade and, spartan as the conditions were, he yearned to set up his billet in one of them, to enjoy a little of that elusive condition called comfort. Apart from that, St. Yves was more central to his scattered force and his monitoring of the same could be effected more efficiently from there.

Then fate showed its hand. An officer ensconced in one of the ruined cottages offered to share with Bairnsfather who quickly moved in and, with this fellow officer, set about improving this "'umble abode". Here he spent his off-duty periods lying around, writing or reading by the light of a flickering candle, or just listening to the sounds of the night outside.

Life and sudden death were indelibly mixed in the front line. A restricting factor for all was that any movement by day was severely curtailed by the application of immediate punishment in the form of shellfire through the auspices of the German observers with powerful glasses on the high ground at Messines. It was an existence far divorced from

The men from the Rosenberg Château Cemetery and Extension now rest in the Berks Cemetery Extension at Hyde Park Corner. (Cameo 8).

The almost hidden remains of the underground shelter just alongside the cemetery at Torreken Farm (Cameo 10).

The modern house on the corner where once stood the cottage where Bairnsfather's 'Old Bill' was born. (Cameo 13).

The impressive Memorial to the American 27th and 30th Divisions stands proudly on the Vierstraat to Kemmel road. (Cameo 14).

Godewaersvelde Military Cemetery where Nurse Kemp is buried. The Mont des Cats makes up the skyline behind. (Cameo 16).

A Canadian's-eye-view of La Petite Douve Farm seen here from the banks of the La Douve stream where the 7th Battalion bridged it. (Cameo 17).

reality, although for him and thousands of others it was reality.

It was at night after his gruelling patrol around his posts that his mind needed stimulus. He pondered the options open to him. Reading and letter writing could only consume a certain amount of time and, as a diversion, he called on his talent for sketching. He was soon scribbling his expressions on the conduct of the war on any piece of material he could lay his hands to. To the delight of his brother officers and men alike, he then pinned these little works of art to the battered cottage walls. Comments on them were passed along the trenchline, frequently with copies of the sketches. He cartooning skills became well known, acting as a tonic and morale booster to oft-sagging spirits, providing a safety valve for the tensions of everyday life. His interpretations of the absurd situations in which he and his comrades found themselves triggered the sense of humour of those who came in contact with them.

It was within his ruin of a cottage where he spent so many winter nights that the inspiration for an explosive formula came about which was to change his life for ever. His sketches embraced officers and men alike. They expressed misery, hardship, discomfort, moans, groans, awful conditions, indigestible food and other subjects close to the heart of the British front-line soldier. All they needed was a catalyst, a central character to take the brunt and utter the opinions, suggestions, complaints and heartfelt misery of the ordinary bloke in khaki who felt the whole world had picked on him as a target for its problems.

So arose from the Flanders mud the grizzly figure of Old Bill, casting his shadow over all and sundry like a latter-day Goliath.

115

Bairnsfather's work was soon a dinner-table topic in brigade and divisional messes. Using Old Bill as a vehicle, he would capture events of the day, transforming them into illustrations – a shell-burst near the cottage forcing the occupants to scamper about for cover; a near-miss from an enemy sniper; qualities inherent in army issue biscuits; a sentry's attire to keep damp from his freezing bones; comments and attitudes of men carrying out daily fatigues or their remarks about an order they felt wasn't quite what it should be – there was plenty for him to get his teeth into, or, more to the point, get Old Bill's teeth into.

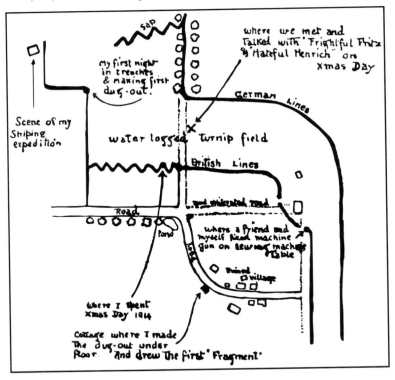

The shell-burst incident received his early attention. A quick sketch captioned *"Where did that one go?"* finalized his first masterpiece featuring Old Bill. Colleagues gave it their whole-hearted approval and at dinner one evening it was suggested he could do worse than send it to the *Bystander* magazine in London. Bairnsfather was not enthusiastic about the suggestion but sent off the sketch and forgot about it, to be pleasantly surprised when, within weeks, a letter from *Bystander* came up with the mail. "We like it; here's a cheque for two pounds and do you have any more?" was the general gist of the response.

That was all he needed. He finalized one on a sniping incident and standard issue biscuits, captioned them respectively : *"They've evidently seen me!"* and *"Chuck us the biscuits Bill – the fire needs mending!"* and off they went. They were snapped up by the magazine whose readership reacted favourably. This led to a regular contributions resulting in what was later to become *Fragments from France* making Bairnsfather fame and fortune in the process. Old Bill, the grumpy unruly-haired private peering over the top of the trench, took his place in the British armoury, a role he filled throughout the war.

Old Bill remained in the hearts of soldiers and civilians alike, but Bairnsfather himself moved north with his regiment and marched into the Second Battle of Ypres. He went into action with the Warwickshires and was badly wounded by shellfire between St Julian and Mousetrap Farm on a day which saw his regiment lose over 500 officers and men.

He was invalided to England and his road to recovery was long and hard, his war as a front-line soldier over.[4] He had contributed more than most to the final victory by letting loose Old Walrus Face on the battlefields of France and Flanders.

His own description of his beloved creation can hardly be bettered as it passed into perpetuity :

First discovered on the alluvial deposits of South Flanders.
Fed almost exclusively on jam and biscuits.
Hobbies: filling sandbags on dark, wet and windy nights!

Notes :

1. One of Bairnsfather's fellow officers was a Bernard Law Montgomery, later to find fame in another war as Montgomery of Alamein, designer of the famous victory in 1942. He had been wounded early in the war when, in October 1914, he was sniped by a marksman located in the village church steeple of Meteren near Armentières. Montgomery would reappear in this same area of Ploegsteert 26 years later when in 1940 he organized and fought the defence of the Comines Canal near Ypres to assist the British retreat to Dunkirk.

2. The Christmas Truce of 1914 is documented in detail by Bairnsfather in his book *Bullets & Billets* which includes a picture of him at St Yves besides the remains of a pond. Not much of St. Yves remains today but the pond is still there, the corner where the cottage stood is still there, the field where the football match took place is still there and, for those who think deep enough and stay long enough, Old Bill is still there.

3. Hill 63 is the high ground west of St Yves and Prowse Point, surmounted by the ruined Château of La Hutte. It was the extreme western limit of Bairnsfather's nightly tours to the west when checking his machine-gun posts. Two small mine craters are to be found alongside the road linking St. Yves to Hill 63. These were the result of the explosion of the mines heralding the opening of the Messines offensive in June 1917, destroying enemy strong-points sited there. .

4. Bairnsfather had a troubled career after the war, gaining a certain popularity and fame in the world of show business when he wrote and directed several theatrical properties based around his wartime character Old Bill. He died in 1959 after a long and gruelling illness.

118

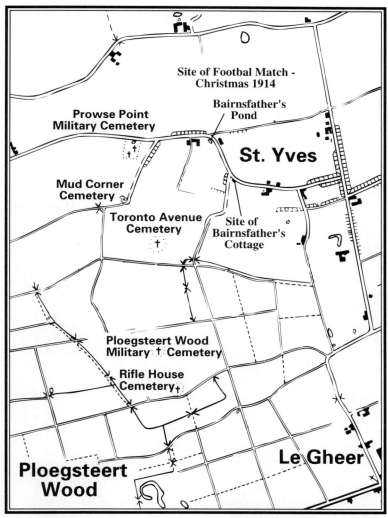

The eastern edge of Ploegsteert Wood as it is today. The pond mentioned by Bairnsfather in front of which he had his photograph taken (as seen in *Bullets & Billets*) is still there but his cottage was completely destroyed during the conflict. Today a newly built modern house takes its place on the corner of the little road leading to Hill 63.

Photograph : Ted Smith

Looking toward the Vierstraat Ridge which was the objective of men of the American 27th and 30th Divisions on August 31st to September 1st 1918.

Its a long way to Berlin,
but we'll get there
Popular American song in 1917.

14

THE YANKS ARE COMING!
First action at Vierstraat, Ypres, 1st September, 1918.

A N IMPOSING MEMORIAL TO THE FIRST American involvement in
the Ypres Salient during the Great War stands on the
left of the road from the village of Vierstraat to Kemmel.
Erected by the United States Battlefield Monument
Commission in 1925, it records the capture of the Vierstraat
Ridge during the period 18th August to 4th September
1918. Two American divisions were involved, the 27th
(New York) Division commanded by John F. O'Ryan, a
lawyer from New York, and the 30th (Tennessee) Division
under the command of Edward M. Lowis from Nashville,
Tennessee. In 1918 both divisions found themselves
attached to the British Second Army for schooling in trench
warfare methods and disciplines, the 27th headquartered at
Douglas Camp, Abeele, and the 30th at Vogelte Farm, close
to Poperinghe due west of Ypres.

This system of acclimatization was to prove successful,
forging bonds of friendship which stood troops from both
continents in good stead in the days to come. Except for a
few instances of confusion with language and signal
procedures, plus a few minor complaints about the quality
of British army rations, the Americans settled in well and
the battle-hardened British veterans were impressed by the
attitude, approach and enthusiasm of the new arrivals.

Both divisions had been bloodied in skirmishes and

patrol actions prior to their attachment to the British. Nevertheless they both lacked experience in warfare as practiced in the northern sector of the Western Front and training and instruction were essential if they were to establish their presence as a force to be reckoned with amongst their peers. Throughout the summer of 1918 they assisted in manning the Poperinghe Line, a defensive system protecting the towns of Ypres and Poperinghe from the south. They were responsible for the line in front of Kemmel and the Scherpenberg.[1]

At the end of August 1918 German armies in the north began to shorten the salient they created with their spring offensive across the River Lys. Allied resistance had stiffened and in some areas had reverted to the offensive. Intelligence, noting movements in the enemy lines, particularly the withdrawal of units from Mont Kemmel, decided to reconnoitre tactically important areas to consolidate their overall position and establish platforms for launching future actions. To help secure the British flank south of Ypres an operation was set up to investigate the situation at the villages of Vierstraat and Voormezeele and the ridge of high ground nearby. Subject to the success of this probe-in-strength the plan was to attack and occupy the positions. The probe was to be on the 31st August followed by an attack on the 1st September. The 27th Division's objective was to take the ridge with the 30th securing their flank by occupying Voormezeele and the Lock No. 8 position on the Comines Canal.

The tactics used proved to be singularly successful, particularly suited to troops inexperienced in battle. Artillery bombardment was minimized and, instead of the usual massed infantry onslaught, groups of skirmishers isolated and cut off enemy strong-points in the line which were later mopped-up by dedicated attacks from selected directions rather than from a frontal assault.

The 27th Division's attack force were in contact with the main body of the German 105th and 106th Infantry immediately they breasted the ridge at Vierstraat. They encountered heavy machine-gun and rifle fire but, with a verve and enthusiasm unnerving to the defenders, they were soon in amongst the enemy lines and by 4 p.m. on the 1st September they had achieved all the plan's objectives, taking the ridge and occupying the village of Vierstraat itself. On their flank the 30th Division, although involved on a smaller scale, rigidly adhered to the strict timetable set by II Corps staff and occupied the village of Voormezeele and the Lock No. 8 position exactly to plan.[2]

It had been a successful day for the Americans and, by nightfall on the 1st September, British command would have been reassured in the knowledge that these young men from the New World were capable of delivering all that could be expected of them. The Germans had a few ideas of their own to test the reflexes of the newcomers. They launched a counter-attack at Lankhof Farm on the Ypres-Kemmel road, but men of the 30th Division repulsed this without difficulty before consolidating and settling into their newly-won position until relieved by British units on the 3rd September. They then returned to their respective headquarter camps at Poperinghe to rest and refurbish.[3]

They had given a good account of themselves in their first major action but had taken heavy losses in winning their spurs. On a small parcel of land between 31st August and 3rd September they suffered over 2,000 casualties. Of these, 350 died in combat or succumbed to their wounds.[4]

123

The 27th Division lost 1,300 men and the 30th 800, the greater part due to lack of experience and uncurbed enthusiasm. Sections of the 27th had launched frontal onslaughts on enemy machine guns manned by determined operators who in many cases had been specially selected to sell their lives dearly rather than surrender. Only enthusiasm and lack of experience would cause troops on the Western Front to consider such folly against a foe such as the German army of that time.

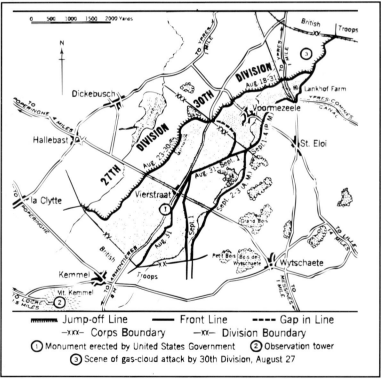

American 27th and 30th Divisions in the Ypre-Lys offensive, August 18th to September 4th, 1918.

In the late summer of 1918 Field-Marshal Haig's evaluation of the units was of the highest order. He judged men of the 27th Division as of superb quality but with a need to control their natural enthusiasm for a fight, which led them to heavier losses than necessary. This was a fault not completely rectified by late autumn when they saw action at St. Quentin, with dire results. As for the 30th, the Field-Marshal's enthusiasm knew no bounds! One report says : "The 30th became the American apple of his eye".

Although not adhering to British-style military bearing and behaviour out of the line, Haig looked beyond this and saw their potential as an efficient and worthy addition to his command. Whilst under constant political pressure to return them to the American forces attached to the French in the south, he strove to retain them under his command. His desire was diametrically opposed to that of General John Pershing, commanding the American Expeditionary Force in Europe. He wanted all American forces under his command as the Franco-U.S. alliance was to be involved in major operations in the Argonne sector near Verdun. He had anticipated Haig's request and put his case with stubborn determination before reluctantly conceding. Field-Marshal Haig resisted the politicians with equal persistence and the 27th and 30th Divisions continued to serve with the British until the end of hostilities.

On the 27th September the two divisions, with their British and Australian allies, attacked The Knoll, a heavily defended strong-point on the St. Quentin canal, a sector of the Hindenberg Line. Although successful, the Americans cast aside all they had learned in Flanders. Battle experience was discarded and they took severe casualties, particularly so on the 27th's front. The trail they had blazed in the glare of inexperience in the Ypres Salient matured in the furnace of battle at St. Quentin. Their baptism of fire was at Vierstraat and Voormezeele, but their coming of age was at The Knoll on the St Quentin Canal.[5] They absorbed the lessons learned in Flanders and on the Hindenberg Line and proved it when, in a set-piece battle alongside the British and Australians, they captured the fortress of Nauroy on the other side of the St. Quentin canal, helped break the defences of the Beaurevoir Line and the Selle River, to arrive on the 1914 battlefield at Le Cateau as the final shots of the war were fired in November 1918.

They had travelled far in a short space of time and had learned their lessons the hard way, but learned them well.

Although the bodies of many of the 50,000 American servicemen who died in the primarily European conflict of 1914-1918 were taken home for reburial in the United States, there are many who rest in the American cemeteries in France and Belgium. The young Americans who lie in those at Wareghem in Belgium and Bony in France; so many miles from their families and homeland, are mute testimony of the American nation's contribution to the final victory in a European war. Let us hope that their countrymen, and those of nations who welcomed their support in those horrific days, do not neglect their sacrifice and keep their memory forever bright.

Extracts from various reports .

107th Inf. 27th Div. USA
The British veterans soon took their American cousins under their protective wing during the summer of 1918.

Near "Scottish Wood" in the "Poperinghe Line", the men of the 107th and the 11th Queen's (British) Regiment were formed into two provisional battalions known as Battalions A & B. It was thought a smoother fusion of the Allies would take place in this fashion. The British were to remain here for two weeks or so, being there to aquaint the men of the 107th in the heterogeneous detail of trench life. They found the young Americans aptly swift and keen to learn all the tricks of life at the front. The numerous phases of trench warfare were passed on, and both British and Americans took every opportunity to fraternise, and a sound bond developed between them, a respect that was to stay with the 107th for the rest of its term in Flanders and France. "Time was spent swapping yarns and cigarettes, and discussing the relative attractiveness of the French madamoiselles and the girls back home."

When the attack on the Vierstraat Ridge at the beginning of September 1918 began, the men of the 107th soon proved themselves worthy adversaries, despite their newness to trench warfare. A platoon of company 'L' which had been in reserve slightly to the rear, charged over the top in broad daylight, and into the front line to bolster their front line comrades. The men took up positions on the fire steps, and with machine gun, bomb, and rifle, inflicted heavy punishment on enemy troops trying to probe the mettle of the newly arrived Americans.

Corporal Randall Henderson received the British Military Medal and Private George Delahay a divisional citation in this action. They were the first men of the 27th New York Division to be decorated and cited for gallantry in action in Flanders and the European theatre.

30th USA ("Old Hickory") Division, Cassel, June 1918
The British who had borne a heavy blow in sustaining the terrific German attack of March 1918 were anxious to have the training of our troops accelerated as much as consistent with sound military practice. On June 11th 1918 they suggested to Second Corps Headquarters that a portion of Phase 'A' training might be completed to advantage by attaching American regiments to British Divisions in the forward zones.

About the middle of June, word filtered through that the

127

Germans were massing forces for an attack immediately east of Cassel. General Herbert Plumer commanding the British Second Army requested the views of our Second Corps HQ as to the assignment of two American Divisions (ourselves and the 27th New Yorkers) to his tactical disposal in the event of a serious hostile attack on the British front. The Corps staff stood firm on their original proposal of non-interference in the orderly pursuit of our original training plans, to suit us for a new life at the front. They signified that in their opinion no real emergency did threaten, but if one did materialise, the matter would be reconsidered by the American Second Corp authorities. The expected attack did not occur, and the training of the Division proceeded on schedule, in the general locality of the Epeleque Forest. In the final stages of its training, the Thirtieth Division enjoyed the distinction of visits by illustrious visitors.

Sir Douglas Haig, the celebrated British Commander, was so impressed with what he saw, he congratulated them on their progress, and on his recommendation to General Headquarters, the Thirtieth Division was one of those he requested to be allowed to remain with the British Army.

General Pershing inspected the Division on June 30th, and also liked what he saw, so much that he allocated some of his best staff officers who travelled with him and jocularly known as "The Travelling Circus", to relocate with the Division with whom they served with distinction.

King George himself came to see the former "Colonials" on August 6th in a car with a miniature Royal Standard. The Sovereign was surrounded by a posse of high ranking British and American officers. A witness notes: "We gave a snappy salute and a cheer, then after an inspection and a smile, the little man was gone"!

The days of long arduous training were now over, and the men of the Thirtieth were ready as they could be. They would be ready when called to take their place alongside their British, French and Belgian allies at the beginning of the great advance that was to rout the German Army from its almost impregnable

Pen & Sword Books Limited
FREEPOST SF5
47 Church Street
BARNSLEY
South Yorkshire
S70 2BR

2

Leo Cooper

Would you like to receive information about other Pen & Sword Books?
Please fill in your name and address below:

Mr/Mrs/Ms ....

Address ....

.... Postcode ....

Please use block capitals

Trade enquiries please tick []   Telephone: 01226 734555

Please tick your areas of interest:

Pre World War One	[]	World War Two	[]	Regimental History	[]
Napoleonic	[]	Post World War Two	[]	Military Reference	[]
World War One	[]	Falklands	[]	Military Biography	[]

positions along the Western Front. The call came on August 15th 1918 in General Army Order 338.

1) The 33rd (British) Division (less Artillery) will prepare to be relieved by the incoming 30th (American) Division. (Guns will be left to support the new Division). This changeover will take place in the area south of Poperinghe/Ypres along the newly prepared East Poperinghe Defensive Line.

The Thirtieth were now at the war!

William F. Clarke, *104th M.G. Company 27th Div. USA, 12/8/18*
We marched up the road from the little airfield at Abeele directly toward Mt. Kemmel in single file. Five paces apart, each gun team behind its limber which carried gun, tripod and ammunition. The track carried heavy traffic in both directions to and from the Battle Line. From time to time we had to disperse to the safety of the roadside ditches, as German fire of the heaviest calibre searched out the back area. As we neared Hallebast Corner and again at La Clytte the firing was continuous. It was after midnight when we arrived at the base of the Scherpenberg, a lofty eminence which dominated the valley to Kemmel.

Half-way up the slopes were a number of dug-outs, the command posts of the units defending this sector. These dug-outs were quite large, dug into the slope of the hill, and reinforced with concrete brick.

We could now see Mt. Kemmel in the moonlight. It seemed very close. An accurate shell would occasionally wing over. There were bursts of machine gun fire, and snipers were active. We could obviously be seen in the clear light. Kemmel was for a time in the enemy hands, and to the British it was like a bee in one's bonnet. It was a damned nuisance to be there, and it sure could sting!

On the night of August 18th we were relieved by an English machine gun squad, and we started back slowly to Abeele. Each of us with his own thoughts and experiences of the past week. We were tired. We were dirty. There was also now an unrelenting determination to get this dirty job over and done with. There was little conversation as with heavy slouching feet we made our way along the dusty road to Abeele. When we arrived, the rest of the company were there, but there were gaps, we had taken losses. We no longer seemed the carefree fellows who had arrived. Our losses and experiences of the past week had a very sobering effect. There were fewer smiles on our faces! When we left the district shortly after to head south to the Hindenberg Line, we sadly left some of ourselves at the little English airfield.

Notes :

1. Concrete dug-outs used by the 27th Division's machine-gun units still exist on the Scherpenberg, a hill near the village of Locre in Belgium..

2. War returned to this part of Belgium in 1940. Lock No. 8 was to see action again 22 years after men from Tennessee rebuffed the German counter-attack following the capture of the Voormezeele ridge. It was in this area that the British 3rd Division conducted a defence of the canal line in assisting the retreat of the British Expeditionary Force in its efforts to reach Dunkirk and evacuation after the German onslaught through France and Belgium.

3. The enemy counter-attack on the 30th Division's position at Lankhof Farm in Sept. 1918 was the closest he came to Ypres in that dramatic year. An Invader Stone was erected here to commemorate the event. British concrete shelters still form a part of the farm's complex today.

4. Some of the first Americans casualties at Ypres in the Aug.-Sept. 1918 actions were buried in the British plot at Abeele airfield, south of Poperinghe. In 1925 they were reburied in the Flanders Field American Cemetery in Wareghem. The area where they were originally buried at Abeele has been left empty as can be seen today. Only two Americans are still buried in the Ypres Salient, both in Lijssenthoek British Military Cemetery near Poperinghe. One was killed in 1918 when on traffic duty in the village of Watou west of Poperinghe by one of the very last long-range German shells to fall in the Ypres Salient .

5. The Americans took nearly 700 casualties in the attack on The Knoll, St Quentin Canal in September 27th 1918. These and other U.S. casualties from French battlefields in the north are buried at Bony American Military Cemetery near Vendhuile on the Somme.

The ground the American 27th and 30th Divisions covered in late August, early September 1918 in their offensive on the Vierstraat Ridge has changed little today. The ridge ittself has seen changes due to the natural expansion of the villages in the area, particularly Vierstraat itself, but, with a little imagination, the visitor standing by the American memorial and looking eastward will get an excellent idea of what the Germans saw on the afternoon of August 31st, 1918.

Photograph : Ted Smith

The slight water-filled indentation in the ground identifies the site of the mine that exploded in 1955. This photograph was taken on the Warneton road (looking over to Ploegsteert Wood in the background). The mine's twin is believed to be on the other side of the road (slightly north and to the right of where this photograph was taken).

What are you doing, Sentry,
Fresh-faced and brown?
Waiting for the mines, Sir.
Sitting on the mines, Sir,
Just to keep them down.
Lieutenant E. A. Mackintosh – *War, the Liberator.*

15

THE LOST MINES OF MESSINES
Le Pelerin, Ploegsteert Wood, Messines Ridge, 1915-1955

A SPRAWLING COMPLEX OF defensive trenches and dug-outs known as the Birdcage located at the eastern edge of Ploegsteert Wood on the southern slope of the Messines Ridge was an area that had been held by the Germans since 1914. It had been developed with the sole purpose of creating difficulty for the British infantry were it to debouch eastward from the wood towards Warneton and Comines.[1] It was so heavily wired that it had prompted an early British unit facing it to describe it as a Birdcage, a name that remained with it for the rest of the war.

In early December 1914 troops of the 4th Division infantry mounted an attack on the Birdcage sustaining many casualties. Those men of the Rifle Brigade and Somerset Light Infantry who fell could not be bought in due to the close proximity of the opposing trench lines and it was not until the impromptu truce on Christmas Day 1914 that an opportunity arose for them to be collected for burial. A meeting between German and British officers in No Man's Land resulted in both sides collecting their dead and having a general get-together where troops from both trench lines, swapped yarns, cigarettes and photographs as well as playing a game of football. Many of the casualties from that December raid in 1914 can be found today in the Rifle House British Military Cemetery located deep within the confines of Ploegsteert Wood.[2]

The British did not attempt to repeat the exercise either in attack or truce form in the years that followed, nor did the Germans try to eject the British from the wood. Small raids were carried out by both sides to keep each other alert, the most serious being the German raid in 1916 on Moated Farm at the north-eastern corner of the wood. Generally speaking the main part of the area remained quiet, both sides using the sector to instruct incoming units in the arts and crafts of trench life, and to keep a wary eye on each other.

This situation remained so until June of 1917 when General Plumer's Second Army sprung a surprise on the enemy by blowing nineteen mines under his defences in what became known as the Battle of Messines.

The Canadian 3rd Tunnelling Company supervised the firing of the mines in the Ploegsteert sector and the main infantry attack was carried out by the 9th Australian Infantry Brigade from trenches just east of Ploegsteert Wood and south of the little River Douve that flowed along the southern slopes of the Messines Ridge.

The most southerly mines exploded on that fateful morning of the 7th June were in two pairs either side of the 9th Infantry Brigade's flanks, the southernmost pair sited at Factory Farm beyond the right flank, tunnelled in from Trench 122 on the eastern fringe of the wood, close to the the hamlet of St Yves of Bruce Bairnsfather's "Old Bill" fame.

The ground to the right of the proposed infantry advance was down a long, open slope and it was believed that this topography would make it difficult for the enemy to mount a counter-attack. Conversely it would mean the

Australians would be exposed to German fire during the advance. Nevertheless, the attack by the 3rd Australian Division, 9th Brigade, was singularly successful, with a minimum of casualties considering the size of the offensive and the forces involved. There is, however, an emotive reminder of this attack just inside the north-east corner of Ploegsteert Wood near the Mud Corner entrance at Prowse Point. A small military cemetery, Toronto Avenue Cemetery, contains the bodies of seventy-eight men of the 9th Brigade Australian Infantry, of which forty are from the 33rd Battalion and twenty-six from the 36th.

These Australian assault troops are all that are buried in Toronto Avenue, a lonely and rather sad little place dedicated to a group of young men who travelled from the far end of the Empire to die in June 1917 under the sun-filled Flemish skies. They joined up together, they travelled together, they laughed and sang together and, in the final phase of their lives, they fell together.

During the assault a particular incident occurred when the 35th Battalion attacked the Grey Farm area, a major strong-point in the German second-line position sited in the ruins of a farm on a slight rise of ground south of the River Douve and just north-east of St. Yves. Undetected machine guns behind the strong-point were causing havoc amongst the oncoming Australians until, one by one, they were disposed of. In one case Private H. R. Sternbeck shot two of the machine-gunners and captured the gun – he was sixteen years old at the time, having enlisted at fifteen and a half years old.

The British had charged four other mines in the proximity of the Birdcage 400 yards further south of those tunnelled from Trenches 121 and 122. It was originally planned to fire them with the rest on the morning of the attack. The decision was altered when it was decided that the enemy, who had proved himself adept in the past at gaining an advantage from the British mining tactics, might do so again, as, with the four most southerly mines, his reserves would be closer to the resulting craters than the British attackers. By occupying the lips of the craters as had been their habit in the past, they would play havoc amongst the oncoming ranks of attacking infantry. It was therefore thought more prudent to hold fire on these mines and keep them, fully charged, for use in some later operations in the sector. As it was they were never used, the enemy retirement from the Messines Ridge and its surrounds after the 7th June causing them to be made surplus to immediate requirements.

With the activity in these sector sbeing of a secondary nature to those greater events taking place in other parts of the front for the remainder of 1917 and all of 1918, the mines east of Ploegsteert Wood were forgotten. In 1918 when peace came and the work of reconstruction commenced after the Armistice no further thought was given to these 'Lost Mines of Messines'. The massive charges in their underground tombs would have possibly remained slumbering giants for all time, but, by a quirk of coincidence, one of them was set off during a particularly heavy thunderstorm in the summer of 1955.[3]

Electrification had been bought to this rural Belgian district during the 1940s and 50s and one of the pylons carrying the power lines had been erected on ground overhead of one of the old 1917 charges. This pylon was struck by lightening triggering the mine beneath. After thirty-eight years of inactivity it roared into life, causing not

136

a little surprise and concern to the local population.

Thankfully there were no casualties, but the damage was extensive. A large section of the land, ditches, and country road was gouged out by the eruption, leaving a large crater which would have soon filled with water as land depressions in this part of Flanders are prone to do. The local authorities moved promptly and efficiently to repair the damage, filling-in the smoking crater, reconnecting the electrical supply and allowing rural life to proceed normally without too much interruption to its traffic and daily routine.

The mine had erupted in a field on the secondary road which skirts the eastern fringe of the vast wood before turning in an easterly direction towards Warneton. No traces of the crater exist today although aerial photos show clearly its perimeters lying about seventy-five to 100 metres along the road to Warneton as it bends away from the wood.

Tom Gudmestad, a dedicated American researcher of the Great War, was in the area in recent years and interviewed a local resident living where Trench 122 and the mine shaft feeding the Birdcage mines had been located. This particular resident had been working in his garden at the time of the explosion. By counting off the pylons from the corner of the road where it followed its course from the wood in the direction of Warneton, he indicated precisely where the explosion had taken place. After a heavy rainfall, a depression in the field retains water and highlights the slight shallow formed from where the earth filling the crater has subsided and settled, the only trace left of a noisy day in 1955.

The sister mine sleeps on undisturbed, approximately

150 metres to the north of this innocent shallow in a cultivated field. For the sake of this rural backwater and its inhabitants working away in fields disturbed only by noise of tractors, harvesting equipment and the odd passing motor car, let us hope it remains so. As for the two remaining, these mementoes of those allied tunnelling companies who worked so hard to place them were mentioned by the official Australian historian C. E. W. Bean in his *Official History of Australia in the War of 1914-18, volume IV, The A.I.F. in France 1917,* but no documentation comes easily to hand to corroborate their position or even their existence.

So much for the Lost Mines of Messines.

Notes :

1. The Birdcage was one of those rare areas of the Western Front which never changed. Both sides held sternly to their positions here from October 1914 until the spring of 1918 when the Germans occupied the wood briefly.

2. Rifle House British Cemetery can only be reached from the northern end of the wood via Mud Corner Cemetery. Any other route is frowned upon by the wood's custodians due to most of the wood area being a preserve for the rearing of game.

3. At the corner of the road where the 1955 mine blew, the Germans established a strong-point called German House. It was captured and destroyed by the lst Battalion Rifle Brigade in December 1914, one of the objectives of the famous attack by 11th Brigade on 19th December 1914. German House was destroyed and never rebuilt. A photograph of it can be seen in *The History of the Rifle Brigade, Vol. I, 1914 -1916* (facing page 44).

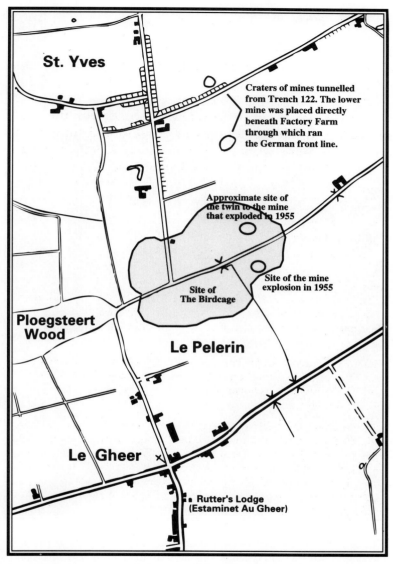

St. Yves

Craters of mines tunnelled
from Trench 122. The lower
mine was placed directly
beneath Factory Farm
through which ran
the German front line.

Approximate site of
the twin to the mine
that exploded in 1955

Site of the mine
explosion in 1955

Site of
The Birdcage

Ploegsteert
Wood

Le Pelerin

Le Gheer

Rutter's Lodge
(Estaminet Au Gheer)

East of Ploegsteert Wood the peaceful rural nature of the area makes it
difficult to imagine the happenings of 1917 and 1955.

139

Photograph : Ted Smith

The old stationhouse at Godewaersvelde no longer services the needs of passengers, whether in peacetime or war, from the railway line which once ran alongside. Today it acts as a schoolhouse for juniors in this peaceful little agricultural town on the borders of France and Belgium.

140

In Flanders fields the poppies blow
Between the crosses, row on row ...
John McCrae.

16

HOSPITALIZATION SOUTH OF POPERINGHE
Belgium 1915-1918

THERE ARE NEARLY 200 British military cemeteries in the
Flanders province of Belgium which accommodate the
250,000 men of Britain and the Empire who fell here
during the Great War of 1914–18. A large proportion of
these men are commemorated on the many Memorials to
the Missing for those who have no known graves.
Together they testify to the commitment and sacrifice made
by Britain and others in defending this corner of Belgium.

Circling the town of Ypres like a vast white-studded
green and brick-red mantle, they are beautifully
maintained by the Commonwealth War Graves
Commission and bear eloquent and silent witness to the
equality in death afforded to men of the Empire who fell
whilst in the service of their country, whether of noble or
humble birth and irrespective of race, colour or creed. In
France the story is much the same and an activity carried
on throughout the war years emotively and physically links
these two countries at one of their border crossing. This
was the care, attention and transportation of the wounded
from the Flanders battlefields in Belgium to the hospital
bases on the coast of France.

Two cemeteries, one on either side of the Franco-
Belgian border, hold a particular poignancy for the
relatives and friends of those who lie within, for these

141

contain not the bodies of men who died in the heat of battle. They are of those who had survived all that, were wounded and passed through the regimental aid posts and the advanced dressing stations to be collected by field ambulances for further treatment and transportation to the back areas for hospitalization in the casualty clearing stations there. Also therein lie the bodies of men who fell sick in the abnormal conditions into which they were thrown in the demands of war and men who were wounded by a stray shell or a spent bullet whilst going about their duties in the reasonably safe back areas away from the dangers of the front line. Common to most of them is the fact that they died while under the care of those tireless men and women of the medical arm of the great war machine. Others who lie here are registered as killed in action, and they were, in that they were employed in the administration and the transport of men and materials feeding the never-ending supply lines snaking from the French coast to the front line. They would have met their fate through the long-range shell or the marauding enemy aircraft and its deadly load.

The cemeteries, at Godewaersvelde in France and Lijssenthoek in Belgium, lying serenely in the then back areas of the Ypres sector, differ markedly in shape and size, but both illustrate the compassionate work of the Commonwealth War Graves Commission. They lie along the route of the old railway line between Hazebrouck and Poperinghe, part of the main communication line from the army bases to the Flanders battlefields.

At Lijssenthoek, a small hamlet aside the Boeschêpe spur road leading southwards off the main Poperinghe-to-Steenvoorde road, a military cemetery houses 10,770 casualties from all parts of what was then the British Empire and from America, France and Germany, and the grave of an old soldier who worked for the Imperial War Graves Commission in the post-war years.[1] Lying beyond the extreme range of enemy shellfire Lijssenthoek was a natural position to set up clearing hospitals and with them the railway sidings necessary to facilitate the collection of the more severely wounded for transport south to the sophisticated hospitals on the French coast and thence, if thought desirable, across the Channel to "Blighty".

Lijssenthoek was first used as an hospitalization area by the French Hôpital d'Evacuation, but in June 1915 it began to be used by the British for their casualty clearing stations and, between June 1915 and August 1918 it became the site of the second largest British war cemetery.[2] April to August 1918 saw the withdrawal of the casualty clearing stations from this area ahead of the German advance, with both British and French field ambulances taking their place. The 658 French graves in Lijssenthoek give testimony to this critical period of 1918.

A large percentage of the British casualties who lie in the cemetery would have succumbed to their wounds after having been bought in from the trench lines further east , using the comprehensive transport system set up to carry them directly from regimental aid stations close to where they were wounded. In spite of the efficiency of this system many would not withstand the journey and by the time they were rushed to the waiting surgeons and compassionate nursing staff at the medical complex they were past hope. Lijssenthoek was hardly the best place to expound the glory of war as the ever-growing ranks of wooden crosses at the time would testify.

143

Some of those who did survive the jolting of the pavé roads would receive vital medical attention before being placed in a general ward for rest and recuperation. Others would have their dressings changed, be treated with whatever medication would best help them suffer their pain before entraining for their journey to the coast and the better equipped base hospital facilities at Boulogne, Etaples, Paris Plage and Danne-Camier where medical services were as good as any in the United Kingdom.

The railway sidings around Lijssenthoek, identified by the troops at the time as Remi Sidings after the name of a large farm in whose grounds most of the medical complex was sited, formed part of the transport system link from Poperinghe passing through Lijssenthoek, Abeele and Godewaersvelde and then on through Hazebrouck and southwards to the French coast. Remi Sidings was embraced within the large area around Poperinghe which saw continuous activity in the daily routine of the numerous transport forms that transgressed this part of the country : motor transport moving men, materials and supplies up the line; field ambulances delivering their sorry loads before moving back toward the front to collect more; rail-freight traffic bringing in more men and materials to feed the avaricious war machine, and the ever-busy hospital trains loading and moving their charges away from the area to more sophisticated coastal medical zones.

Although out of range of enemy gunfire the continuous road and rail activity attracted more than enough attention from the enemy in the air. The German air force mounted frequent air raids across the area extending as far south as Godewaersvelde and Steenvoorde causing considerable casualties amongst the long-suffering wounded as well as

144

the other military personnel and medical staff.[3] The raids were condemned by the allies but protests were rebuffed by the enemy who, although recognizing the existence of hospitals in the area, classed it as being a legitimate military target by virtue of the system of rail-lines being used to bring in men and materials as well as its close proximity to several military airfields housing Royal Flying Corps scout and observer squadrons. The railways *were* used for transporting men and materials and the nearby airfields at Abeele and Proven *did* house the said squadrons, so what more could be said? The air raids continued throughout the critical months of the Passchendaele offensive in the summer and Autumn of 1917 and into the winter of 1918, reducing in intensity once the enemy perceived his fortunes to be on the wane, but nevertheless adding to the row upon row of wooden crosses filling the burial plot alongside Remi Farm.

The area where most of the sad and painful activity of loading casualties on to the ambulance trains is noted today for its long rows of hop poles standing in silent uniformity, whilst the cemetery itself on the other side of Remi Farm guards its complement of men.

Not much remains of the many barns and buildings which housed these men during their short period of life as patients. The places of limited freedom and enjoyment where they could enjoy banter and conversation with kindred spirits, indulge in a sing-song, generally relax and feel free from the war and the extreme conditions of the cold Flemish winters have gone forever. Those who were well enough to explore the environs of Remi Sidings and mix with the men and woman who served by doing their duty in the back areas were well catered for. Whether their companions were doctors, nurses, medical orderlies or hospital administrative staff, or yet transport drivers, railway officials, stores personnel, clerks, ordnance men, pioneers, engineers, or any other members of the massive military organization supporting the allied war effort in the back areas, the local population, never slow to exploit a commercial opportunity, ensured places of cheer. Weak beer was sold to the thirsty hordes at exorbitant prices; egg and chip merchants operating out of rural homesteads did a roaring trade and *Estaminet* became a soldier's word for a place providing something of a substitute, although a poor one, for part of the life they had left behind. On cold winter evenings many of these establishments resounded to the raucous singing of lusty young voices as described by Edmund Blunden enjoying a camp concert held in a barn close to Remi Sidings in 1917.[4]

As well as Lijssenthoek, the nearby villages of Abeele and Boeschêpe vibrated to the nightly sound of men enjoying themselves, experiencing a brief interlude from the harsh realities of their life and the horrors of war.

Hardly anything remains to indicate what happened during those traumatic times. Remi Farm (Remi Houve as shown by the sign on its gateway) still separates the cemetery from the old railway sidings, acting as a landmark and allowing reflection on the location which gave its name to a place so necessary yet so unwanted in the serious business of war. Only the insensitive who visit here as the Flemish light begins to fade can fail to perceive the hosts of wraiths that people this particular Silent City remaining to inhabit this quiet and misty region.

Part of the railway embankment which expedited the shuttling of wounded humanity now supports a road linking Poperinghe to Steenvoorde. It is in constant use by a generation of motorists too intent on their daily business to be aware of the bustling, sometimes dangerous, but always tragic events that took place in the vicinity of the farmstead edging their route.

To return to the activity of that time, an incident is captured in the diaries of an American surgeon, a medical volunteer from Harvard University operating with a British military ambulance unit. He details the death of Edward Revere Osler, an officer of British and American parentage serving in 1917 with A Battery, 59th Brigade, Royal Field Artillery. Revere Osler, the son of London surgeon Sir William Osler, had been seriously wounded by shellfire on the Steenbeek River near St Julien, Ypres. The diarist was a friend and colleague of Sir William.[5]

Thursday, August the 30th, Dozinghem Cemetery

Last Sunday came a letter from Lady Osler telling me that Revere was somewhere near St. Julien and how dreadful it would be should he be brought in to me with a head wound, and yet how thankful they would be. I answered immediately, asking her to wire me the number of his unit so that I could try and locate him among the millions. Rather used up, I was preparing to turn in at 10 last night, when came this shocking message : "Sir Wm. Osler's son seriously wounded at 47 C.C.S. Can Major Cushing come immediately?" The C.O. let me have an ambulance, and in a pouring rain we reached Dozinghem in about half and hour. It could not have been much worse, though there was a bare chance – one traversing through the upper abdomen, another penetrating the chest just above the heart, two others in the thigh, fortunately without a fracture.

The local C.O. would not let me cable, and I finally insisted on phoning G.H.Q. – got General Macpherson on the wire and persuaded him to send to Oxford via the London War Office: "Revere seriously wounded: not hopelessly: comfortable.".

Crile came over from Remi with Eisenbrey, and after a transfusion, Darrach, assisted by Brewer, opened the abdomen about midnight. There had been bleeding from two holes in the upper colon and the mesenteric vessels. His condition remained unaltered, and about seven this morning the world lost this fine boy, as it does many others every day.

We saw him buried in the early morning. A soggy Flanders field beside a little oak grove to the rear of Dozinghem group – an overcast, windy, autumnal day – the long rows of simple wooden crosses – the new ditches half full of water being dug by Chinese coolies wearing tin helmets – the boy wrapped in an army blanket and covered by a weather-worn Union Jack, carried on their shoulders by four slipping stretcher-bearers. A strange scene – the great-great grandson of Paul Revere under a British flag, and awaiting him a group of some six or eight American Army medical officers – saddened with the thoughts of his father. Happily it was fairly dry at this end of the trench, and some green branches were thrown in for him to lie on. The Padre recited the usual service – the bugler gave the "Last Post" – and we went about our duties. Plot 4, Row F."[6]

The death of Edward Revere Osler provided a strange link between the battlefields of Ypres and those of the American Revolutionary War of 1775. A tenuous link perhaps, but a link nevertheless. Paul Revere's clarion call-to-arms in 1775 began the war which gained the colony its independence.[7] What would that old firebrand have thought of one of his descendants being buried on a European battlefield draped in the union flag and wearing the uniform of the British King.

In 1915 when the British arrived south of Poperinghe to use the area as a base for its casualty clearing stations, Godewaersvelde, just across the border in France, had already outgrown its rural village origins and was now a town supporting around 6,000 souls. Towering above the town was the imposing Mont des Cats, one of the highest features on the borderland between France and Belgium. At the crest of the Mont des Cats sat the Trappist monastery housing a community of priests and brothers active in looking after the needs of the local people.[8] To the east, the larger town of Steenvoorde controlled the French border crossing, much as Abeele fulfilled the same function in Belgium to the north. To the British troops pronouncing the name Godewaersvelde caused them a problem which they soon solved by angliciszng it to a more acceptable "God Wears Velvet".

Like the large hospital complexes across the border at Lijssenthoek and Abeele, Godewaersvelde was on the military railway running south from Poperinghe towards the railhead at Hazebrouck and on to the coastal hospital facilities to be found around Boulogne. As such it became a vital link in the chain and developed an importance of its own in affording care and attention to the wounded at the beginning of their long and painful voyage back to the coast. Numbers 37 and 41 Casualty Clearing Stations, both set up close to the village and the railway line, were made ready to be operational and to receive the influx of injured humanity expected as the bruising military campaigns of 1917 developed.

The fields and meadows alongside the small station house of Godewaersvelde were soon bustling with the activity surrounding these facilities, and the clearing stations became operational within a very short space of time.[9] Huts were built, tents erected, wards and operating theatres were constructed and in June of 1917, just before the opening of the Messines offensive, Number 11 Casualty Clearing Station joined the complex, making three hospitals ready to operate just to the north-east of the little town as a back-stop, or overflow support, to the expected casualty influx at Lijssenthoek and Abeele. As the casualties flooded into these two, the overflow facilities at Godewaersvelde were to become indispensable to the overall treatment and care of the wounded and soon proved their worth.

During the long hot days of that dramatic summer, many seriously wounded men began their long and often painful trek by rail south towards the coast where the medical help available would be at its most sophisticated level. Many of the wounded were unable to withstand the shock of their injuries or the trauma of the journey and would be removed from the hospital trains at selected locations en route for further medical attention or, so tragically for many, immediate burial. The cemetery at Godewaersvelde was started just after the Battle of Messines to meet this latter need.

Places of mass suffering have a momentum of their own, and Godewaersvelde was to be no exception to that rule. Between the summer of 1917 and the Spring of 1918 over 700 young men of Britain and the Empire would find their last rest in this remote part of rural Flanders, swelling to 968 after the Armistice due to the gathering of bodies from local battle-area graves, always to be found where once the war machine had rested.

The tragic scenario of burying the dead after removing them from the trains was played out on an almost daily basis at emotive spots on the journey south from Poperinghe to Hazebrouck, itself a sizeable town used as a British military base since the early days of the war and, as such, harbouring major hospital facilities of its own. Apart from the cemetery at Godewaersvelde others sited near station halts, like those of Gwalia Farm near Poperinghe, Trois Arbres at Nieppe, and Bailleul Ambulance Sidings at Bailleul, were used for the same purpose.

The long hospital train with the Red Cross emblem displayed on the sides and tops of its carriages would arrive at these halts amid the hissing of steam and grinding of wheels. On stopping, the scene would change to one of frenzied activity as sweating orderlies worked at top speed to complete their duties ensuring that the train with its pitiful cargo could proceed with the least possible delay. The work of mending broken bodies was commenced immediately by the waiting doctors and nurses whilst, for those cases where human intervention was too late, a hastily arranged but sensitive committal service was conducted by the burial party under the dutiful but sympathetic eye of the camp chaplain.

In such a fashion then did the burial plot alongside the casualty clearing stations at Godewaersvelde begin, and in a locale which had witnessed no land fighting at all, nor had experienced any bombardment except for a brief period in the Spring of 1918 during the Germans' last desperate attempt to break the British line.[10] Once an insignificant backwater but now of strategic importance on the rail link south, Godewaersvelde figured prominently in the military planning for assisting the wounded. It represented in the starkest possible terms the cost in human sacrifice in one small section of the Ypres sector of the Western Front. Such was the symbolism embodied by Godewaersvelde, its experience being sadly typical of several hundred similar locations behind the old front line from Nieuport on the North Sea coast to the frontiers of Switzerland 300 miles to the south.

When the first British units moved into the Franco-Belgian border area during 1914, the rural tranquillity of the local country appealed to them, and they soon settled into their new surroundings. Many of the more discerning officers amongst these units realized that this period of respite would be brief enough. Time perhaps to acclimatize the new men into life under active service conditions, implement some aspects of training and allow the younger soldiers, new to the front line, to experience their first taste of life in the field. Once this honeymoon period was over, it would be strike camp, fall in all sections, and head, in orderly procession, northwards towards Ypres and the firing line. The flickering flashes and low rumble of gunfire in the evenings spelt out that the prospects for a quiet life such as recently experienced were to be considerably lessened in the Ypres sector.

"I do miss home mother... it is quiet enough during the day ... but in the evenings it does get noisier and we can hear the guns like the thunder up north (Ypres) Please don't worry though ... we are quite safe here!".

So wrote a young Irish soldier, Private Sylvester Cahill, to his mother in London whilst he was at rest in the Spring of 1915 with the 3rd Battalion Middlesex Regiment.[11] By the time his mother received that encouraging note from her youngest son she had already lost him, killed in action during an abortive attack near the infamous Mound at the village of St Eloi south of Ypres.

At Godewaersvelde, as in other locations billeting British units, many of the troops at the time felt that the local population, far from welcoming them as erstwhile liberators, resented their presence in such large numbers and viewed them with trepidation.

This may have been unfair and not always compatible with the truth, but there is no denying that some observers who served with the British referred to the dour character of the host community who, although never slow to exploit the commercial opportunities presented the large captive clientele billeted on them, were at the same time never at ease with the military strangers who had disrupted the normal flow of their peaceful rural life.

Several unit histories referring to time billeted at Steenvoorde state that : "The natives were distinctly unfriendly". It was at Steenvoorde and Godewaersvelde that the story generated of certain farmers having locked their water pumps to stop British troops using them, and that water and fresh forage, so vital and necessary for the hundreds of military horses using the area, were being sold to the British at exorbitant prices. The farmers, given the chance, probably would have quoted chapter and verse on the misuse and abuse by British troops of the valuable commodities of fresh water and clean forage. Not being of inexhaustible supply, it was difficult enough to eke out an existence for themselves without being prey to the illicit demands of an alien army who thought it within its remit to use and commandeer what it liked. No wonder that military claims officers were frequently called upon to negotiate a satisfactory settlement between an irate farmer and the sometimes abrasive and not always understanding military personnel. The native population sometimes found it difficult to take to heart the allies with all their attendant customs and strange humour, often wickedly offensive as only soldiers can be. A typical example was recorded by Lieutenant F. C. Curry, an infantry officer serving in the locality during the early summer of 1915. His diary notes :

It was rather a wretched day we spent in this little farm. Heavy rain had turned the orchard in which we lay into a real bog, and all the straw we could beg, borrow, or steal from the inhabitants could not keep us out of the mud. Here too we found the first instance of friction between the troops and the civilian population and the old lady at the farm made no bones about telling us how unwelcome we were. She opened hostilities by taking the rod from her pump so that we could not fill our watercart, and the troops retaliated by stealing bundles of unthreshed wheat. This was speedily put a stop to (and paid for) by the officers, and for a while peace reigned whilst she did a growing trade with cups of coffee and glasses of weak beer.

Then one day, some of the officers saw some fresh baked bread in a little room off the kitchen, and offered to buy some. To our surprise, the old dear started to wave a knife around dangerously and screamed at us : "You take my wheat, you take my water, and now you won't even leave me my bread. I would rather the Germans were here... at least they pay for what they take". As we had just paid for all her straw we thought that a bit thick, and pointed out if the Germans were here, we would fear for her safety and that of her two slatternly daughters doing a roaring trade with the coffee and beer among the troops thronging the farm. This at least quietened the old lady down and she saw our point!

There were instances which illustrated the reverse. Godewaersvelde was practically untouched by enemy shelling, but his air force was active over this part of France through 1917.[12] A survivor of one air raid in October of that year, Nurse June Catherine Macfie, when interviewed in recent years, recalled that dramatic night in detail and gave a startling observation on the locals of Godewaersvelde :

Q. What about lights in the ward?
A. They'd be paraffin lights.

154

Q. Yes, but how about blackout?

A. Oh, they'd put down the lights at once when the bombing came over, not a light to be seen.

Q. That must have been difficult.

A. Well, while it was going on it was just silence ... patients and nurses, we were all shaking, you know ... naturally, when they came over. We were all frightened, it was so near, and the men were frightened too.

Q. Did they show it?

A. Well, I suppose they did, but they tried to be awfully strong, you know, and brave. One terrible night we were struck and there were two casualties, but at the next CCS a Sister was just going on duty and she was killed on the spot, and five patients were killed and about 100 wounded. And the sister and the orderly were buried at Godewaersvelde, and the whole village turned out, all dressed in black. Of course, all of France was in mourning anyhow, and they all followed the cortège to the grave. It was very nice of them, wasn't it?

Q. Did the nurses go as well?

A. Some of them. Yes, I went.

Q. Did you know that Sister?

A. No, Sister Kemp was her name. I just knew her name.

Q. And was that in your cemetery she was buried?

A. Not in our CCS, the next one.

Q. And do you remember that night of the bombing?

A. Oh yes! I was on duty through the night. We'd just started you know.

Q. Was there a siren or something or some kind of alarm?

A. No ... you just heard bombs dropping and that was all.[13]

The sympathetic picture of the whole village turning out in black to pay tribute at the burial service hardly reconciles with the image of a hostile population as recorded by soldiers at the time and, that apart, Godewaersvelde Military Cemetery still embraces the bodies of over 1,000 men from Britain and the Empire who never went home, who never made it beyond the little railway station in the village. They remain there with the final message of young Sylvester Cahill written in 1915 echoing faintly down over the years : "Please don't worry Mother ... we are quite safe here".

We know they are. God rest them at God Wears Velvet.

Notes :

1. Lijssenthoek Military Cemetery is the second largest British military cemetery in France and Belgium, second only to that of Tyne Cot. It contains the graves of :

   7,350 from the United Kingdom and Ireland
   1,131 from Australia
   1,053 from Canada
   291 from New Zealand
   29 from South Africa
   21 from the British West Indies
   5 from Newfoundland
   2 from India
   3 from the United States of America
   3 whose country of origin is unknown
   656 from France
   223 from Germany (wounded prisoners of war)
   1 ex-soldier who worked for the Imperial War Graves Commission

The Americans who lie here are unique. All other Americans who fell in Flanders were re-buried in the Flanders Fields American military cemetery at Waregem on the road to Brussels. One of those buried at Remi Sidings, on traffic control duty at the village of Watou west of Poperinghe in the Autumn of 1918, was killed by one of the last long-range shells to fall in the Ypres sector.

2. The Remi Sidings medical complex at Lijssenthoek comprised :

 July 1915 to April 1918 –   No. 10 Casualty Clearing Station.
 Aug. to Sept. 1917 –   No. 13 Casualty Clearing Station.
 July 1915 to April 1918 –   No. 17 Casualty Clearing Station.
 Last months of 1918 –   No. 62 Casualty Clearing Station.
 No. 10 Stationary Hospital was still operating in November 1919

3. Four bombs fell on No. 17 Casualty Clearing Station at 9.20 p.m. on

17th August 1917 killing twenty-seven of whom thirteen were German prisoner patients. Thirty-nine others were badly wounded.

4. Edmund Blunden, the poet and writer, served with the Sussex Regiment in the Ypres Salient during 1917.

5. Sir William Osler was born in Canada in 1849 and was one of the leading medical lights of his day, influencing medical men and opinion on both sides of the Atlantic in London, Toronto and Baltimore.

6. Second Lieutenant Edward Revere Osler is buried at Dozinghem Military Cemetery, Westvleteren, Belgium. Plot IV, Row F, Grave 21.

7. It was Paul Revere who made the famous ride in 1775 from Boston to Lexington Green to warn the gathering colonials in rebellion that : 'The redcoats are coming".

8. Later in the war the infamous hospital "caring" for those patients with self-inflicted wounds was opened on the Mont des Cats. Many of these would have found their way to this hospital from the Casualty Clearing Stations at Godewaersvelde, Abeele and Remi Sidings.

9. The station house, now a school house and no longer serving a railway, still stands close to the cemetery.

The Godewaersvelde medical complex comprised :

July to November 1917 –	No. 37 Casualty Clearing Station.
July to November 1917 –	No. 41 Casualty Clearing Station.
July 1917 to April 1918 –	No. 11 Casualty Clearing Station.

10. The cemetery at Godewaersvelde, begun on July 1917 after the Battle of Messines, contains the graves of :

893 from the United Kingdom
65 from Australia
4 from Canada
2 from New Zealand
2 from South Africa
1 from India
19 from Germany (prisoners who died of wounds)
1 Sister of the Territorial Force Nursing Service

Apart from those bodies from the casualty clearing stations, there are those buried by the field ambulances and fighting units who used the plot from April to August 1918 during the German offensive. Five graves are of men of the 110th Brigade Royal Field Artillery who were brought in from a point near the Mont des Cats (Plot II, Row AA). A large French burial plot existed on the terraced land at the higher end of the cemetery in May and June 1918 but these graves were moved after the Armistice.

11. Private T. S. Cahill, 3rd Btn. Middlesex Regt, aged 19, K.I.A. the 31st March 1915 at St. Eloi, lies in Voormezeele Enclosure No. 3. near Ypres. Plot II, Row B, Grave 19. He is also remembered on his parents, grave at Kensal Green Roman Catholic Cemetery, North London.

12. Main air raids on Casualty Clearing Stations during the period July-November 1917 :

Date	Hospital	Location	Casualties
4th July	No.1 CCS	Bailleul	1 nurse killed
7th July	No.11 CCS	Bailleul	23 patients killed and 70 wounded
23rd July	No. 2 CCS	Trois Arbres	2 RAMC and 2 patients killed and 20 wounded
5th Aug.	No.46 CCS	Gwalia Farm	2 RAMC and 1 ASC killed, 25 ASC wounded
16th Aug.	No. 3 CCS	Brandhoeck	1 Doctor and 1 RAMC killed
7th Aug.	No. 17 CCS	Remi Sidings	6 RAMC, 8 Soldiers and 13 German prisoners killed. 40 various wounded
21st Aug.	No. 44 CCS	Brandhoeck	1 nurse killed
20th Oct.	No. 37 CCS	Godewaersvelde	1 nurse killed, 8 RAMC and 7 patients wounded

Air raids on hospitals and casualty clearing station at Dozinghem, Westvleteren in this period killed 24 and wounded 105.

13. Acknowledgement with gratitude is given to Lyn Mcdonald for permission to quote her taped interview with Miss Catherine Macfie regarding the air attack on Godewaersvelde which appeared in her book *The Roses of No Man's Land* published by Michael Josephs Ltd (1979). Nurse Kemp, killed during the raid on the hospital, is buried in Godewaersvelde British Cemetery. Plot I, Row K, Grave 1.

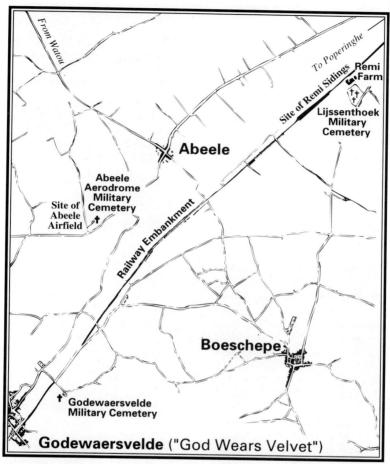

The railway line running from Poperinghe to Hazebrouck has long ceased to exist. The railway embankment can still be followed from Lijssenthoek (Remi Sidings) Military Cemetery in Belgium to the stationhouse at Godewaersvelde (today a schoolhouse) just across the border in France. That part of the embankment in Belgium is now a busy road leading from Poperinghe to Steenvoorde. This road sits atop the embankment until Abeele on the Franco-Belgian border from where it changes course due west to Steenvoorde, leaving the embankment to continue its old route on to Godewaersvelde.

159

La Petite Douve Farm taken from the bridge crossing the River Douve. The road to Messines is to the right of the farm with the distinctive tower of the church visible on the skyline. It was immediately north of this bridge that the Germans built their barrier, which the Canadians dispensed with by firing an 18-pounder at it from point-blank range.

"That beastly little ruin"
Dr C. E. W. Bean.

17

CANADA AT YPRES
La Petite Douve Farm, Messines, November 1915

A T THE OUTBREAK OF THE Great War in August 1914, the
Germans fielded questionably the most powerful
military machine in the world and displayed a standard of
battlefield efficiency far in excess of the armies of the
allies. More by good luck than by military judgement did
the alliance keep in the game as the enemy flowed across
Belgium and northern France carrying all before them.

In November 1914 the war of movement following the
German retreat from the River Marne and the Aisne ground
to a halt, resulting in trench lines extending from the
Belgian coast to the Swiss frontier. The British and French
armies in the Ypres sector of the Western Front found
themselves holding the low ground around the old
Flanders town with the Germans ensconced on the ridges
of high ground around it. Thus became established what
was to become known as the Ypres Salient.

To the south of this salient was the Messines Ridge with
a farm situated on its southern slope commanding a
position overlooking the ground which any allied attack
from the direction of northern France would need to cover.
Its position endowed it with a strategic importance and the
German command transformed it into one of their strong-
points, named on their battle maps as *Weihauchtshof.*
Immediately below it was the leafy mass of Ploegsteert

Wood and, behind the wood, Armentières just across the frontier in France itself. The River Douve winding its leisurely course across the southern slopes of the ridge gave its French name to La Petite Douve Ferme. Twice was this farm to flicker into prominence finding a place in communiqués of the time, first in 1915 and again in 1916 before it finally fell to men of the Anzac Corps at the start of the Messines offensive in June 1917.

In October 1915 the Canadians were responsible for this area and, until then, there existed a live-and-let-live attitude on both sides of No Man's Land. The 2nd Infantry Brigade, 1st Canadian Division, set about changing all that, quickly and dramatically too. The enemy's 11th Reserve Infantry Regiment were the farm's garrison at the time and, safe and snug as its troops felt in their deep trenches, a rude awakening was shortly to be meted out to them.

Although the main actions for 1915 were over, British High Command decided the coming winter would not pass in idleness on the Canadian front. A Second Army directive stressed that "passive defence" would not be practiced and that the winter months would be spent in training and acclimatization to trench life in anticipation of future operations, and to generally lowering the morale of the enemy. Short, heavy bombardments would be a regular ploy to keep the enemy in a constant state of alert, sniping was to be developed to a fine art, and trench raiding, introduced by the British during the previous summer, would be activated on a regular basis.

Comprising anything from ten to a hundred men, a trench raiding party's objective was to effect a quick, entry into enemy trenches, inflict casualties, take prisoners and documents for identification purposes, and return swiftly to its lines. The Canadians took to this with enthusiasm. The blacking of faces, the dulling of metal surfaces, then moving out, lightly armed into the night appealed to them, giving scope for inventiveness which they relished, rekindling the old North American frontier spirit.

The first in-strength trench raid was recorded in the Spring of 1915 just before the Canadian Corps entered the Ypres sector. Carried out by a hundred men of the Princess Patricia's Canadian Light Infantry, it was repulsed at the Mound, a feature of ill repute near St Eloi just south of Ypres, incurring sixteen casualties, five of them fatal.[1]

A raid on a grander scale would be attempted by men of the 5th Battalion (Saskatchewan) and 7th Battalion (British Columbia), 2nd Infantry Brigade, in the early morning of the 17th November 1915. Their target was the front-line trenches around La Petite Douve Farm. The objectives were threefold: 1) secure prisoners for interrogation; 2) destroy dug-outs and capture documents and 3) persuade the enemy's 11th Reserve Regiment that something big was afoot and to encourage it to call up reserves to man the trenches, thus preparing a first class target for the British artillery shoot timed to follow the raid.

The raid was nearly two weeks in its preparation under the control of Lieutenant H. Owen of the 7th Battalion. Rigorous training began after the selection of five officers and eighty volunteers from the 7th and a similar number from the 5th. They were excused all other battalion duties as they practiced the moves that would be expected of them, especially the forging of a fast-flowing, deep stream with specially prepared bridging ladders, due to heavy rain having swollen the River Douve to nearly three times its normal width.[2] They were also schooled in the use of protective matting designed to ease their route over any wire defences they should encounter on the way.

The German line north of the river jutted out from the farm creating a salient in the Canadian line over 500 yards in length before crossing the Messines-Ploegsteert road. The section along the edge of the road from the farm to the river was the target for the 7th Battalion, supported by a diversionary attack by the 5th 1,000 yards to the east, across the flooded Douve. Aggressive patrolling in the days leading up to the raid had ensured that every detail of the sector was recorded and also caused the resident 11th Reserve Regiment to withdraw its screen of sentry and listening posts, offering the advantage of surprise to the forthcoming raiders. The day prior to the raid British and Canadian 18-pounders pummelled the farm and its wire defences and, during the evening, trench mortars added their weight to the onslaught on the enemy garrison, now hunched and apprehensive in their muddy holes.

Before the raiders moved into their setting-off positions all identifying items were removed and Ross rifles were exchanged for the more efficient Lee-Enfield. Black crepe masks were handed out, primarily as camouflage but also to present a ghoulish, fearful presence which, coupled with the surprise of the attack, would add a thoroughly terrifying aspect to the already shell-battered and weary enemy. The masks also served as a form of identification to the Canadians in that, in the dark trenches, anyone not showing a black face was a target for extinction. If this wasn't enough, some of the raiders had attached powerful torches to their rifle barrels to dazzle and confound the defenders when they met them in the narrow trenches. The enemy wire surviving the day-long bombardment had been cut by special pre-raid parties and, at precisely 2.30 a.m. on the morning of the 17th November, in the light of a full moon not accounted for in the raid plan, both raiding parties set out towards the enemy lines, in parallel but separated by a space of about 500 yards. Almost immediately the 5th Battalion were in trouble as they encountered a thick bank of German wire hitherto unobserved which lay along a ditch en route to their objective. Their leading elements became badly entangled and struggled with great difficulty to disengage themselves. The enemy on this front, now thoroughly aroused, opened fire and, although well short of their objective, the 5th Battalion troops were forced to retaliate with rifle and hand bombs. Things were falling apart on their front in spite of the careful planning of Lieutenant Owen.[3]

To the left front the 7th Battalion party had reached their objective, quickly and silently moving along the river edge to the small bridge that carried the main Ploegsteert-to-Messines road across the stream. The marauders swiftly scaled the road embankment and fell upon the unsuspecting enemy forward posts. Finding little resistance, the Canadians sited bombing blocks, wire and sentries on their flanks to repel counter-attacks, although none as such materialized. After half-an-hour the raiders withdrew, achieving all their objectives and killing or wounding thirty of the enemy. As the sky began to lighten they took back with them to the Canadian lines twelve prisoners for interrogation. Apart from gathering a deal of vital information from across the way, a bonus for the allied intelligence officers was the opportunity to examine a new design of gas mask recently issued to the enemy troops.

The Germans retaliated with a hastily mounted infantry

attack against the Canadian front but this was effectively dispersed by allied artillery, waiting for just such an opportunity to inflict more casualties on the enemy. The 7th suffered one man killed when his rifle snagged on the wire and he was shot in the struggle to free himself, and one other was slightly wounded.[4] The 5th had been unable to overcome the wire in the ditch but Lady Luck smiled on them as, in good visibility in full view of the enemy, they returned to their lines without loss.

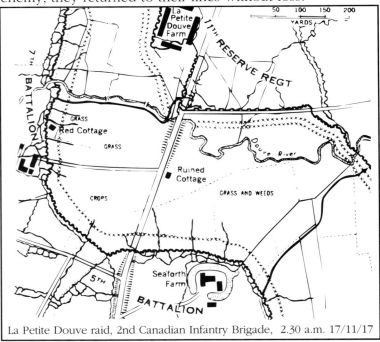

La Petite Douve raid, 2nd Canadian Infantry Brigade, 2.30 a.m. 17/11/17

The Canadian and British commands later referred to the action as a "model raid" and a blueprint for future ones.

Several weeks later at the same bridge the 5th were

again in action, this time to dismantle a timber barricade erected by the enemy in advance of his line. The Canadians bought an 18-pounder up to their own line and, at point-blank range, fired twenty-six rounds at the obstacle. A minor infantry assault was mounted and the barricade was swept away in the face of little opposition. The enemy garrison was either killed by the shellfire or captured by the Canadian infantry who followed it. Two men of the 5th were wounded in the action.

An observer's account, November 1915, Messines Sector
This was the first big raid carried out by the battalion. The theory was that the Germans had been sitting there very quietly. Nothing happened last night, the night before that ... or will happen tonight. This was the thinking on both sides, and Jerry was caught by surprise.

Our scouts organized the whole thing – they sort of ruled no-man's-land led by Lieutenant Owen who did the planning. It took a long time to get H.Q. approval but in the end it came. Some of the N.C.O.'s were Sergeant Ashby, 'Dutch' Kendal, his brother Noel, Fraser (later the company sniper and commissioned in the field down in France). There were several others, Mead, McDirmid, and Captain Holmes who took over from Lieutenant Owen when he went on leave. Captain Holmes did well in the circumstances, because he was not too well acquainted with the general plan. The raiding party went over towards the farm very silently, and the cover party took up their position at their rear. I was one of the four on the alert at the parapet ready to count them all back in.

After the fireworks ended, Captain Holmes came down into the trench and said the boys were bringing back eleven prisoners. But when our count was completed we found they had twelve defected prisoners with them. (One must have given birth on the way.) Sadly though one of the raiders had been lost down by the river bridge, and he was named as No. 429072

Private Mead. [5] We discovered later that he had been hit near the enemy line. Captain Holmes received a medal for his part in the affair, and several of the lads got an award too. When Lieutenant Owen returned from leave to discover the raid had taken place without him, he was very disappointed, and none too happy about it. He was a popular officer and was sadly missed when we lost him on another operation a few months later.

After the raid we went out to rest at a place called Westoutre in West Flanders where we were inspected by the King himself. The Canadian Mounted Rifles took over from us, but they were pretty green, and we soon got called back to find that in our absence, the Germans had cheekily built a fortified barricade on the Messines Road by the river bridge, the scene of our earlier battalion exploit. (The enemy obviously wanted some prior warning of any future raid which might be mounted on the farm defences.) We had to get rid of it, but how if we were to avoid the loss of lives attacking frontally? Finally we got one of our 18 pounders right up into the actual front line, wrapping sand bags around the wheels to deaden the sound on the cobblestone surface. From there we blasted the barricade to pieces from point blank range. Poor old Jerry, he did get a shock!
Private A McGowan, 7th Battalion C.E.F

A raider's account (26.1.1985). November 1915. Messines Sector

From their positions on the forward slope of the ridge, the Germans could almost peer into our firing trench, and the communication trenches leading to the rear. They also controlled the River Douve, a deep creek really which ran from inside their lines into ours. They used to annoy us by damming up the Douve then suddenly releasing the accumulated waters; you can guess the rest! They also had several forward saps and earth barriers acting as observation and listening posts in advance of the lines on the Messines Road, forming a perfect salient which enclosed a battered red brick farm, called La Petite Douve Farm.

The weather turned sour during October and it rained

168

frequently. The Douve became very swollen and soon flooded into our line which became waterlogged. We were surrounded with collapsing walls and a real bog of mud.

On November 8th we were relieved from our misery and retired to slightly drier quarters at Grand Munque Farm. The following morning it was announced that a raid was planned on the German position at Petite Douve Farm to relieve our position somewhat and stir up the enemy.

In a screened field at the side of Grand Munque Farm a small-scale replica of the German trenches had been laid out, and we marvelled at the details finely marked out of the farm and its local defences. Once the plan was outlined and accepted, volunteers were called for and a party was chosen from No. 2 Company. However, we were surprised to discover that the Scout Officer Lieutenant Owen would not be leading the raid, even though the planning was mostly his, compiled on the good work of his scouts. Another officer (Captain Holmes) was placed in charge.

Lieutenant Phillpott assembled us and instructed that Brigade had ordered that communications would need to be maintained throughout the entire raid. The Colonel (Lieutenant-Colonel J . Odlum) would be posted in Trench No. 133 and we were all allocated respective duties. The upshot being I was to be at the official report centre with Captain Thomas in the front line.

For several days we went over the plans meticulously, the group ensuring they knew their task exactly. It was stressed to all concerned that the objective was to break into the German trenches where they cut the road south of the farm, raise havoc and establish Canadian supremacy on this front, the effects to be psychological as well as material. During all this period of preparation, our guns around Grand Munque Farm were firing "special shoots" to harass the enemy and trying to cut his wire.

On the 15th, the entire party moved up into the cellars and shelters at Irish House, a battered-down farm just in front of the Winter Trench. Empty sandbags were distributed and we were told to pack all our kit and personal belongings into these, one for each man. Lieutenant Phillpott supervised this, the orders being very strict to remove any items which would provide identification to the enemy. In addition to our usual trench kit, we took off all badges, our identity discs, and removed letters, pay books, and any paper items which had our name and unit on them. The sandbags were sealed and stacked in the cellar at Irish House. After dark on the following night, the raiding party moved up into Trench 133 from where the raid was to start. Colonel Odlum was already there waiting for us near a breach which had been made in our parapet. Men were out in front of the trench, cutting a path through our own wire. Two scouts came in over the parapet and reported that the artillery had failed to cut the German wire completely and a small team was sent out with cutters to complete the job.

The raiders were all jammed up in the trench, a mass of men, each group carrying its speciality items, two wooden bridges, rifles, shovels, wire, aprons of bombs, and Callahan and I with our telephone and heavy reel of 'phone line. Just before midnight the moon set and Captain Thomas worked his way down the trench, "Get ready men. We're going over." The men had all been issued black cotton masks which they tied over their faces, as much for identification in the German trenches as for concealment. A white face in the enemy system meant "German" and quick extinction. There was a brief flurry of activity in the trench as the masks were adjusted and tied on, caps crushed down, weapons and loads shifted for the exit.

Right at midnight the parties crawled up over the parapet and out through our wire. Sergeant Callahan and I followed out the last group, hoisting the heavy reel of wire into the gap in the parapet and struggling with our rifles and telephone to keep up with the men in front. The ground directly in front of the trench was greasy mud cleared of the usual tin cans and bottles, and we advanced, trailing the black wire, into the gap in our barbed wire.

Following the raiders, we crawled as quietly as possible along the right bank of the Douve, keeping as close to the ground as we could. There was no response from the German trenches and the party remained undetected.

About fifty yards from the Messines road, we could see the road embankment loom darkly in front of us. This screened German observation to the east and it was at this point that the bridges were laid across the Douve. The party had already scrambled across the two bridges by the time Sergeant Callahan and I arrived. We selected a small section of old tumbled-down trench, ran our wire into it, and connected up the D3 telephone. The line was good back to the signal post with Colonel Odlum in Trench 133 and immediately "Shorty" Preston had connected up a line forward, across the bridge to a point where Captain Thomas had set up a command post.

The raiders had disappeared into the blackness ahead of us and all was quiet. Callahan and I lay on the forward lip of our hole, peering into the darkness. I had the phone to my ear and there was only its steady, low hum in the silence. For several minutes there was nothing, no sound, no movement. Then a flash of orange light from ahead and to the right near the road and at a time the muffled crack of a bomb which was followed by another and another. Screams and cries pierced the night and a wild crackle of rifle shots.

At the same time a heavy rifle fire was opened up, right on schedule, onto the German trenches to left and right of the raid, machine guns joined in, and rifle grenades and trench mortars began to burst on Petite Douve Farm further ahead. More bomb bursts could be heard but more muffled and further away.

The Germans fired flares to left and right but none came from in front of us. They fired a few artillery shells but they were obviously confused about the state of affairs and the shells burst behind us, along our old front line. And behind us, to left and right, our front line blazed forth in streaks of red and orange.

For many minutes there was nothing known except the obvious, "Raids gone in". Then, nearly fifteen minutes into the raid, two red flares soared up from the breach in Trench 133, followed by shrill whistle blasts from in front, the signals to "come back".

"Raiders coming back." A dark crowd scurried over the wooden bridge, running now in a dark group. In a breathless mob, they rushed past us booting and dragging a dozen prisoners. More orderly but just as quick came "Shorty" Preston and Captain Thomas with a group of rifleman who had stood by with him as support. When they were abreast of our listening post, Callahan and I jumped up with our disconnected phone and set off at the rear of the party.

More flares went up from the German lines and machine guns started to flash and chatter. There was a sudden, cold downpour of rain that drenched us but failed to dampen the hilarity of the party. The raiders had moved into the front line and then continued back with the prisoners. Following orders, Callahan and I made straight back across the open and reported in at battalion headquarters at La Rossignol. German shells fell sporadically all over the front and it took them half an hour to properly shell our trenches and supports.

The raid has been a complete success, one of the first of its kind on such a large scale by British forces. One raider had been killed and one wounded but twelve prisoners had been taken, several dozen killed, and their dug-outs had been bombed and the defences studied. Its success proved to be a feather in the battalion's cap, many congratulations poured in and decorations were handed out. "Shorty" Preston got the D.C.M. and most of those who entered the German trenches received a special leave to Paris.

The following day, we were relieved again by the 10th Battalion and marched out to Bulford Camp for one night's rest, continuing on to Westoutre the next day for a cushy spell in Corps reserve. We prepared for a promised long duration of rest and refitting, glorying in the attention from the raid.

While at Westoutre, the other signal lance corporal, Andy Faris and I were ordered by Lieutenant Phillpott to spruce ourselves up and to report to the battalion quartermaster. With some effort and with no explanation we cleaned the mud off our tunics and belts, brushed and polished our boots and reported to the quartermaster as ordered. We were joined there by seventy-three other men from our battalion, an honour guard to be inspected by King George V it turned out! In honour of the occasion, the quartermaster's men dished out the first steel helmets, or "tin hats" as we called them. They were stamped out of thin metal, irregularly cut around the brim, and tended to totter rather uncertainly on top of the head. But they were more protection than our cloth hats and once the novelty wore off, we were glad to have them. In fact I used to feel absolutely naked without my helmet on, later in the war.

Sporting the new headgear, our contingent for the honour guard marched off down the road to Locre and there joined similar detachments from other battalions of the 1st Canadian Division. We were lined up by a flock of red-tabbed staff officers, groups of men on either side of the meandering, cobble road.

There was a hush and a snappy "Shun" which brought us all to attention. With no further fanfare, our king appeared, mounted on his white charger. He dismounted, spoke with the officers for a moment and then quietly passed along the ranks, stopping now and then to speak with one of the men. He walked by me without stopping. He was surrounded by a horde of the staff now, but I could see, him quite clearly, a tall, bearded slightly gaunt figure with an air of patient sadness about him. It was thrilling to see him nonetheless.

At the end of the line, he walked back slowly and mounted his horse. Upon a cue from one of the officers, we gave the old boy the traditional three cheers, raising our helmets and making a great row. Unfortunately we must have sported his horse because it reared up and threw the king to the pavement. He was apparently badly hurt. He lay on the ground stunned and was quickly surrounded by his retinue. He was eventually taken away but in the meantime we were hastily bundled off and instructed

173

not to mention the episode to anyone.

We were allowed to keep the steel helmets after rejoining the battalion. Additional helmets were not issued to the battalion for some time and we were the objects of much curiosity and envy amongst our comrades.

Our rest at Westoutre lasted until the ninth of December when we were suddenly marched back to the line in front of Messines, relieving a battalion of newly-arrived Canadian Mounted Rifles. During their stay in our old trenches they had allowed the Germans to erect an advanced post behind a barrier of earth and logs on the Messines road. The C.M.R.s had been unable to demolish the barricade, some of their own men firing on them from Winter trench. In order to put the Germans in their place again, our brigade had been ordered back from rest. The 5th Battalion was to attack the post, our battalion being in support. Fortunately we weren't needed, the 5th Battalion making a neat job of it. But our rest had been completely ruined, there was no return slated to Westoutre, and we stayed in the waterlogged trenches in blasphemous, ugly moods.

A leave warrant arrived with my name on it. In the nick of time I packed my kit and arrived at battalion headquarters to pick up the warrant. L/Cpl. Andy Faris was going on leave too, so we set off together, walking to Bailleul where we caught a train for the coast. At Boulogne we took a steamer for Folkestone, and a train carried us up to London. Andy was going to Dublin to visit some family, and I was going to an uncles at Dundrum quite close to Andy. We had a most enjoyable ten days' leave, made all the more pleasant by the fact that Andy knew someone who worked in the Guinness brewery in Dublin, and we were taken on an "extended" tour of the place, had a great time, and got thoroughly "wet" on the inside. When we arrived back we rejoined the battalion who were still out at Westoutre glorying in the attention from the raid.

The end of the month though brought several changes, and also tragic loss to the battalion. Lieutenant Owen, our fine scout and intelligence officer who had engineered the successful raid on Petite Douve Farm, was shot through the head near Ploegsteert whilst fighting it out with a German patrol in the middle of no-man's-land. He was a man's man, a soldier's soldier, greatly respected and a heavy loss to the battalion. (His father was a well-known cleric from Victoria B.C. His devoted scouts bought his body in, and he was buried in our little regimental plot at Red Lodge (Roosenberg Château)".

Pte. E Rossitter, 7th Batt CEF. [5]

So ended the activity around La Petite Douve Farm during 1915. In August 1916 British Command included it in its scheme for mining operations for the attack on the Messines Ridge the following year and tunnellers began to lay an explosive charge beneath it. Enemy engineers suspecting what was going on, burrowed down some eighty feet and found the props supporting the tunnel. They broke into it, only to be met by an explosion of a charge blown by the British who had anticipated the intrusion. Nine enemy sappers were killed. The Germans in their turn later retaliated by blowing some 6,000 pounds of explosives, killing four British pioneers in the process. In view of the resulting damage the British discontinued work on this mine and eliminated its potential for the 1917 offensive. [6] Diverting water from the River Douve, they flooded the complex, thus ending the warlike activities around La Petite Douve Farm. It remained the linchpin of the enemy defences hereabouts until the onslaught by Anzac troops in June 1917 when it was taken on the opening day of the Messines offensive.

This "beastly little ruin", so named by those marauding Anzacs, is today a thriving farm complex on the western edge of the main Messines-Ploegsteert road. [7] The fast-moving traffic plying the road today makes it difficult to stop and ponder at this interesting sector, but it is worthwhile for the visitor to make the effort. The ground over which men of the 5th Battalion (Saskatchewan) and 7th Battalions (British Columbia), 2nd Infantry Brigade advanced remains relatively unchanged. The small bridge is still there and the site of the barricade is easy to locate.[8]

Notes

1. The casualties from the attack on the Mound at St. Eloi in March 1915 by the Princess Patricia's Canadian Light Infantry, including the Commanding Officer, Lt. Col. F D Farquar DSO, are buried in the British Military enclosures at the village of Voormezeele

2. The flooding around the Canadian position led to many records and dug-outs being lost. The 16th Battalion C.E.F. History records a response for information from headquarters as "lost in the flood'", an excuse they were able to use on a number of such occasions..

3. Lt. H. Owen (Vancouver, British Columbia) was killed in action in January 1916 on another raid. He was buried at Rosenberg Château on Hill 63. but later moved to Hyde Park Corner Extensions. While in the front line at La Petite Douve Farm the 2nd Canadian Infantry Brigade buried all its dead at Rosenberg Château Cemetery.

4. Private J. Mead, Regt. No. 429072, was buried by the river but his grave was lost in later fighting. His name is on the Menin Gate at Ypres.

5. Eric Rossitter survived the war. He spent his last years in a retirement home in Vancouver, British Columbia. He died in 1990 aged 93. His ashes were laid by Military Historian Tom Gudmestad (Seattle USA) in Passchendaele New British Cemetery, Belgium, as was his last wish.

6. Of the mines laid to support the Messines offensive 19 were exploded on the morning of the assault. The mine at La Petite Douve Farm was lost, whilst several charges laid east of Ploegsteert Wood were not triggered. One exploded during a thunderstorm in 1955.

7. 'That beastly little ruin' came from War Correspondent Dr C. E. W. Bean in his *The AIF on the Western Front 1916-1918. Volume V.*

8. The timber barricade erected across the Messines-Ploegsteert road was sited north of the River Douve beside the present-day road bridge.

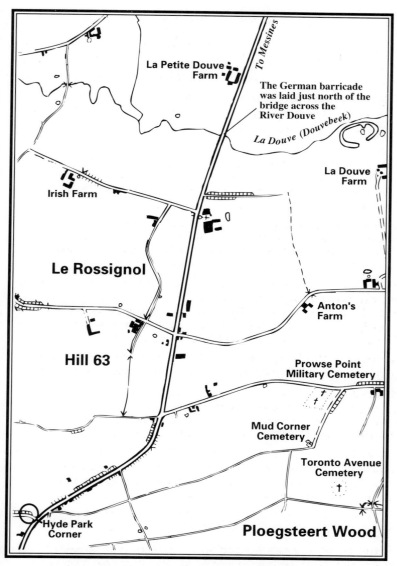

La Petite Douve Farm still overlooks the route to northern France from its position on the southern slope of the Messines Ridge.

BIBLIOGRAPHY

American Armies and Battlefields in Europe. (American Battle Monuments Commission, United States Printing Office. 1938).

The Anatomy of a Raid. A. Spagnoly/E. Smith. (Multidream. 1991).

Armageddon Road. Billy Congreve. (William Kimber, London. 1982).

Australia in the War 1917. C.A. Bean. (Angus & Robertson, Sydney. 1943).

Balliol College War Memorial Book, Volume 2. (R. Maclehose. 1924). ˙

Bruce Bairnsfather. Tonie and Valmai Holt. (Milestone Publications. 1985).

Bullets & Billets. Bruce Bairnsfather (Grant Richards Ltd. London. 1916).

Canadian Expeditionary Force 1914/19. Col. G.W. Nicholson. (Queen's Printers. Ottawa. 1962).

The Doughboy. The Story of the A.E.F. 1917-18. Lawrence Stalling. (Harper & Row. 1963).

History of the Rifle Brigade 1914 -16. R. Berkeley. (Rifle Brigade Club. 1927).

The History of the Somerset Light Infantry. Edward Wyrall. (Methuen 1927).

The King's Royal Rifle Corps Chronicles 1914. (The Wykeham Press. 1915).

The London Scottish in the Great War. Lt. Col. J.H. Lindsay. (Regt. H.Q. 1925).

Over there with O'Ryans' Roughnecks. W.F. Clarke. (Superior. Seattle. 1966).

The Roses of No Man's Land.. Lyn Macdonald. (Michael Joseph. 1980).

The Royal Berkshire Regiment (Princess Charlotte of Wales's). Vol. II. 1914-18. F. Loraine Petre, O. B. E.. (The Barracks, Reading. 1925).

The 13th Battalion Royal Highlanders of Canada. 1914-1919. (R. C. Fetherstonhaugh. 1925)

The Royal Fusiliers in the Great War. H. C. O'Neill O.B.E. (William Heinemann, London. 1922).

The Royal Scots 1914 – 1919. J. Ewing. (Oliver & Boyd. Edin., 1925).

The Silent Cities. Sydney C. Hurst. (Methuen. London. 1929).

A Soldier of England. Leslie Y. Sandes. (J. Maxwell. 1920).

St. Lawrence to the Yser with the Canadian 1st Brigade. F.C. Curry. (Smith, Elder 1916).

South African Forces in France. John Buchan. (T. Maskin Miller, Capetn. 1921).

Trench Pictures from France. Major John Redmond MP. (A. Meldose Ltd. 1917).

War Underground. A. Barrie.(London, Muller, 1962).

The Ypres Salient. John Giles. (Leo Cooper. 1970).

The Ypres Times. Vol. 2., No. 4.October 1924. Ypres League (Gale & Polden, London. 1924).

Private papers. T. Gudmestad. (Seattle).

Private papers. A. Spagnoly. (London).

Private papers. T. Smith. (London).